Poverty and Exclusion

ISSUES

Volume 160

Series Editor

Lisa Firth

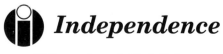 **Independence**

Educational Publishers
Cambridge

First published by Independence
The Studio, High Green
Great Shelford
Cambridge CB22 5EG
England

© Independence 2008

British Library Cataloguing in Publication Data
Poverty and Exclusion – (Issues Series)
I. Firth, Lisa II. Series
362.5

ISBN 978 1 86168 453 0

Printed in Great Britain
MWL Print Group Ltd

Cover
The illustration on the front cover is by
Simon Kneebone.

CONTENTS

Chapter One: Poverty in the UK

Chapter Two: Global Poverty

Useful information for readers

Dear Reader,

Issues: Poverty and Exclusion

In 2005-6, 22% of people in Britain were income poor, living in households with below 60% of the median income after housing costs. Many of these households will contain children, who may never escape from the cycle of poverty and exclusion – current research shows that children from a disadvantaged background can be up to two years behind their classmates educationally by the age of 14. Globally, half the world's population live in absolute poverty on less than $2 a day. **Poverty and Exclusion** looks at poverty in the UK and overseas.

The purpose of Issues

Poverty and Exclusion is the one hundred and sixtieth volume in the **Issues** series. The aim of this series is to offer up-to-date information about important issues in our world. Whether you are a regular reader or new to the series, we do hope you find this book a useful overview of the many and complex issues involved in the topic. This title replaces an older volume in the **Issues** series, Volume 110: **Poverty,** which is now out of print.

Titles in the **Issues** series are resource books designed to be of especial use to those undertaking project work or requiring an overview of facts, opinions and information on a particular subject, particularly as a prelude to undertaking their own research.

The information in this book is not from a single author, publication or organisation; the value of this unique series lies in the fact that it presents information from a wide variety of sources, including:
⇨ Government reports and statistics
⇨ Newspaper articles and features
⇨ Information from think-tanks and policy institutes
⇨ Magazine features and surveys
⇨ Website material
⇨ Literature from lobby groups and charitable organisations.*

Critical evaluation

Because the information reprinted here is from a number of different sources, readers should bear in mind the origin of the text and whether the source is likely to have a particular bias or agenda when presenting information (just as they would if undertaking their own research). It is hoped that, as you read about the many aspects of the issues explored in this book, you will critically evaluate the information presented. It is important that you decide whether you are being presented with facts or opinions. Does the writer give a biased or an unbiased report? If an opinion is being expressed, do you agree with the writer?

Poverty and Exclusion offers a useful starting point for those who need convenient access to information about the many issues involved. However, it is only a starting point. Following each article is a URL to the relevant organisation's website, which you may wish to visit for further information.

Kind regards,

Lisa Firth
Editor, **Issues** series

*Please note that Independence Publishers has no political affiliations or opinions on the topics covered in the **Issues** series, and any views quoted in this book are not necessarily those of the publisher or its staff.*

Poverty: the facts

A summary from the Child Poverty Action Group

What is poverty?

There is an ongoing debate about what 'poverty' means and how to measure it. Peter Townsend offers perhaps the most authoritative definition and emphasises the relative nature of poverty:

'Individuals, families and groups in the population can be said to be in poverty when they lack the resources to obtain the types of diet, participate in the activities, and have the living conditions and amenities which are customary, or are at least widely encouraged and approved, in the societies in which they belong.'

How is poverty measured?

There are many ways to measure poverty – either directly by people's income or material circumstances (including material deprivation, where people lack essential items because they cannot afford them), or indirectly using proxies such as benefit or tax credit receipt and socio-economic classification.

The most commonly used survey data comes from the *Households Below Average Income* series, which provides an analysis of patterns of low income or 'income' poverty. This survey establishes a poverty line, below which individuals are categorised as income poor. The poverty line is defined as 60 per cent of the median household income, adjusted for household composition. It is possible to present data before and after housing costs have been accounted for; the Government prefers before housing costs, because comparable international data exists to allow comparison. CPAG uses after housing costs, because it gives a better indication of disposable income. This definition is used unless stated throughout this summary.

The poverty line in 2005/06 (UK, after housing costs)

Poverty line (£ per week)	
Couple	£186
Single person	£108
Couple with two children (aged 5 and 14)	£301
Lone parent with two children (aged 5 and 14)	£223

How many people live in poverty?

⇨ In 2005/06, 12.7 million people in the UK (22 per cent) were income poor, living in households with below 60 per cent of the median income after housing costs. Though in recent years this has been falling, in 2005/06 it rose. In 1979, 15 per cent were in this position.

⇨ In 1999, the *Poverty and Social Exclusion in Britain* survey showed that 14.5 million people in Great Britain (26 per cent) were living in poverty (defined as lacking two or more 'socially perceived necessities' because they could not afford them). A related survey showed that in 2003, 29.6 per cent of households in Northern Ireland were poor (lacking three or more 'socially perceived necessities' because they could not afford them and having a low household income).

⇨ In 2004, the Families and Children Study found that 8 per cent of lone-parent families and 2 per cent of couple families could not afford to eat vegetables most days (the same numbers were also found for fruit and cakes/biscuits most days). Twenty-one

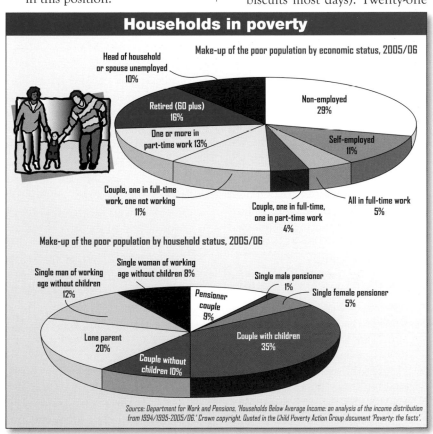

Households in poverty

Make-up of the poor population by economic status, 2005/06

Head of household or spouse unemployed 10%
Retired (60 plus) 16%
One or more in part-time work 13%
Non-employed 29%
Self-employed 11%
Couple, one in full-time work, one not working 11%
Couple, one in full-time, one in part-time work 4%
All in full-time work 5%

Make-up of the poor population by household status, 2005/06

Single man of working age without children 12%
Single woman of working age without children 8%
Single male pensioner 1%
Single female pensioner 5%
Pensioner couple 9%
Lone parent 20%
Couple without children 10%
Couple with children 35%

Source: Department for Work and Pensions, 'Households Below Average Income: an analysis of the income distribution from 1994/1995-2005/06.' Crown copyright. Quoted in the Child Poverty Action Group document 'Poverty: the facts'.

per cent of lone-parent families and 6 per cent of couple families reported that they could not afford new clothes when these were needed.

What causes poverty?

The primary cause of poverty is inadequate income, arising primarily from worklessness, and inadequate wages and benefits. Although it has fallen by 0.1 per cent over the past year, overall employment is high (74.4 per cent) and unemployment relatively low (5.5 per cent) though this is up 0.4% on the previous year. The risk of not being in work, however, varies across groups and is higher for those with low skills, from certain minority ethnic groups (especially Pakistani and Bangladeshi people), and for those living in low employment areas. Other barriers to work include caring responsibilities and discrimination.

Paid work is not, on its own, a guarantee of being free of poverty. Low wages, part-time work and not having two adults in work in a couple household all increase the risk of experiencing poverty. In 2005/06, 57 per cent of income-poor children were in households where one or more parent was in work. Safety-net benefits and tax credits are also often inadequate to protect families with children from poverty, and their value often remains significantly *below* the poverty line.

Who lives in poverty?

Some groups of people have a much greater than average risk of experiencing income poverty.

⇨ Unemployment. Seventy-five per cent of people in households where the adults are unemployed are income poor. When all adults in a household are in full-time paid work, only 5 per cent are income poor.

⇨ Ethnicity. Twenty per cent of White people are income poor, compared with 63 per cent of Pakistani and Bangladeshi people, and 41 per cent of Black or Black British people.

⇨ Household structure. Forty-nine per cent of people in lone-parent households are income poor, compared with 24 per cent of

single people without children. Twenty-two per cent of people in couple households with children are income poor, compared with 11 per cent where there are no children. Sixteen per cent of couple pensioners are income poor. Of those pensioners who are single, 16 per cent of men and 20 per cent of women are income poor.

What is the impact of poverty?

On average, poverty makes people's lives shorter and more brutal than they need be. Poverty is not simply about being on a low income and going without – it is also about being denied good health, education and housing, basic self-esteem and the ability to participate in social activities. It has costs to the individual as well as to society, and by constraining educational attainment it reduces the skills available to employers and impedes economic growth.

⇨ Educational outcomes. Using receipt of free school meals as a proxy for poverty, in England in 2006 60.7 per cent of children not entitled to free school meals obtained five or more GCSEs at grades A*-C, more than double the 32.7 per cent of children who were entitled to free school meals.

⇨ Health. Poverty is associated with a higher risk of both illness and premature mortality. Using social class as a proxy, life expectancy for people in social class V (manual workers) is seven years shorter on average than that for those in social class I. Children in social class V are five times more likely to die in an accident and 15 times more likely to die in a fire than children in social class I.

⇨ Participation. The last *House-holds Below Average Income* series survey asked parents about whether their children had access to a range of items and activities, the report identifies that 7 per cent of children do not have access to leisure equipment (such as a bike), 6 per cent don't have a hobby, 11 per cent can't go swimming, 8 per cent don't have friends round

for tea and 6 per cent can't go on a school trip – all because their parents cannot afford it.

What are the solutions?

'Poverty' is not a neutral term – it implies an unacceptable state about which something must be done. CPAG recommends the following policy changes to reduce child poverty.

⇨ Provide most for those children at greatest risk of poverty.

⇨ Work towards better jobs, not just more jobs.

⇨ Ensure the safety net protects families against poverty.

⇨ Maximise the contribution of child benefit within family support.

⇨ Introduce free at the point of delivery, good quality childcare.

⇨ Make the reduction of child poverty central to the new child support policies.

⇨ Make education truly free at the point of delivery.

⇨ Provide benefit entitlement to all UK residents equally, irrespective of immigration status.

⇨ Reduce the disproportionate burden of taxation on poorer families.

⇨ Improve the quality of delivery and gear it to the needs of the poorest families.

⇨ The above information is reprinted with kind permission from the Child Poverty Action Group. Visit www.cpag.org.uk for more information or to view sources for this factsheet.

© CPAG 2007

Britons lose sympathy for the poor

Information from the National Centre for Social Research (NatCen)

People in Britain are concerned about inequality, but they are less likely to support government interventions designed to tackle poverty or redistribute income than they were 20 years ago. Indeed, according to the latest *British Social Attitudes* report, published today by NatCen, one in four people think that poverty is due to laziness or lack of willpower, up from one in five in 1986.

The report finds that:

⇨ Four in ten people (41%) say that their household is 'living comfortably', up from 24% in 1986. Then a quarter (26%) said that they were finding it difficult on their household income; now only 14% say this.

⇨ Concern about the gap between those on high and low incomes remains high, with three-quarters (76%) saying that it is 'too large'.

⇨ But only a third of people (34%) think that government should redistribute income from the better off to the less well off, down from nearly half (47%) in 1995.

⇨ And few people now see the unemployed as a priority for extra government spending. In 1986, a third of people (33%) chose them as a priority, compared with just 7% now. These changes no doubt reflect an increasing belief that unemployment benefits are 'too high' and discourage people from finding work. In 1986, a third of people (35%) took this view; now over a half (54%) do so.

The public adopt a fairly strict view of poverty:

⇨ A half of people (50%) think that a person is in poverty if they have enough to eat and live, but not enough for other things they need.

⇨ Nine in ten people (89%) think that a person is in poverty if they have not got enough to eat and live without getting into debt.

⇨ The most widely and consistently held view as to why some people live in need, held by a third (34%), is that 'it's an inevitable part of modern life'. But the proportion thinking poverty is due to laziness or lack of willpower has risen – from 19% in 1986 to 27% now.

Professor Peter Taylor-Gooby, co-author, comments:

'These results show a continued decline in sympathy for spending on the poor, and suggest that a part of this decline reflects changing social values about the moral obligation of government to redistribute. These sorts of values are hard ones for governments to influence.

'This raises a dilemma for a government committed to achieving sharp reductions in poverty, when such policies appear to run counter to the direction of social values.'

Note

This summarises 'Trends in sympathy for the poor' by Peter Taylor-Gooby and Rose Martin, in *British Social Attitudes: the 24th Report*, published by Sage for NatCen.
23 January 2008

⇨ The above extract is taken from *British Social Attitudes, the 24th report* produced by NatCen and published by SAGE, and is reprinted with permission. www.natcen.ac.uk

© *NatCen*

Monitoring poverty and social exclusion 2007

Key points

⇨ Overall poverty levels in 2005/06 were the same as in 2002/03. Child poverty in 2005/06 was still 500,000 higher than the target set for 2004/05.

⇨ The unemployment rate among the under-25s has been rising since 2004, while the rate for those over 25 stopped falling in 2005.

⇨ Half the children in poverty are still in working families.

⇨ The number of children in working families where earnings and Child Benefit are insufficient for them to escape poverty goes on rising.

⇨ Overall earnings inequalities are widening.

⇨ At least a quarter of 19-year-olds lack minimum levels of qualification.

⇨ Not all those who want to work can do so, and disability rather than lone parenthood is the factor most likely to leave a person workless.

⇨ The value of social security benefits for working-age adults falls ever further behind earnings.

⇨ Half the poorest households lack home contents insurance, the same as in the late 1990s when first identified by the government as a priority.

⇨ 1½ million children in poverty belong to households that pay full Council Tax.

⇨ The public sector is the largest employer of low-paid workers aged 25 or over.

December 2007

⇨ The above information is reprinted with kind permission from The Poverty Site, maintained by the New Policy Institute and their sponsors, the Joseph Rowntree Foundation. Visit www.poverty.org.uk for more.

© *New Policy Institute*

Missing school trips makes you poor, say British kids

Information from Community Services Volunteers

New research charting the attitudes of children to poverty in Britain shows that nearly half of all young people think missing out on school trips or not having the correct school uniform are the most telling indicators of being poor.

The research also reveals that a fifth of children think having a mobile phone is just as important as having a book to read at home. The survey also finds striking differences in the attitudes and experience of young people in different parts of Britain.

The research was commissioned by the Dare to Care: Make time to help end child poverty campaign and records the attitudes of children aged 7-16 towards poverty in this country. The specialist research involved face-to-face interviews with more than 700 children and was conducted during the summer by independent children's research agency, LVQ.

The research is designed to underline how communities and individuals can make their own mark in helping to combat child poverty in this country through volunteering. Dare to Care aims to recruit 35,000 volunteers from October 2007 through to March 2008 to help combat child poverty.

Key findings

⇨ Nearly half of children (44%) think that not being able to afford to go on a school trip is a sign of poverty.
⇨ 2 out of 5 children (40%) think that not having all the correct school uniform makes you poor.
⇨ Nearly a third of children (28%) think not being able to give a present to a friend at a birthday party is a sign of poverty.
⇨ A quarter of children say that going to school without breakfast (23%) or not having a safe place to play nearby (24%) makes you poor.
⇨ A fifth of children told researchers that not having a mobile phone (19%) or books to read at home (20%) can indicate poverty.

Regional variations

⇨ 78% of children in the North East felt not having a place to play safely was a sign of poverty compared to a UK average of 25%.
⇨ 47% of children from East Anglia and 37% of children from London think not having a mobile phone makes you poor (UK average – 19%).

A fifth of children told researchers that not having a mobile phone (19%) or books to read at home (20%) can indicate poverty

---

⇨ 58% of children in the South West think not being able to give presents at a friend's birthday party makes you poor compared to a UK average of 28%.
⇨ 31% of children from the West Midlands and London consider not being able to use a computer to do school work is a sign of poverty (UK average – 18%).

Dare to Care is run by CSV, the UK's leading volunteering charity and the Campaign to End Child Poverty, a coalition of 90 organisations. Around 1 in 3 children (3.8 million) live in poverty in the UK, many well below the poverty line. The UK has one of the worst rates of child poverty in the industrialised world but efforts to change this can be successful.

Hilary Fisher, Director of the Campaign to End Child Poverty, says: 'It is interesting that for children it seems the visible indicators of poverty are the ones that they are most sensitive about. Not being able to afford to go on school trips or the correct uniform leads to uncomfortable questions from their peers and in some cases can lead to bullying.'

A fifth of children told researchers that not having a mobile phone can indicate poverty

Sue Farrington, Director of Corporate Affairs at CSV, said: 'People throughout the country have enormous potential to use their skills, time and energy to respond to what children are telling us are important indicators of poverty. Volunteers can run breakfast clubs, improve the reading skills of children, support families with debt, mentor pupils who are bullied and create safe places to play. Giving time can help end the poverty of experience that far too many children face in this country.'

To find out more about the Dare to Care campaign visit: www.daretocare.org.uk

LVQ Research interviewed 727 children aged 7-16 through face-to-face interviews between 16-23 August 2007. *19 September 2007*

⇨ The above information is reprinted with kind permission from Community Services Volunteers (CSV) and the Campaign to End Child Poverty. Visit www.csv.org.uk for more information.

© CSV/Campaign to End Child Poverty

Britain's forgotten poor

More than one in six of UK's working population 'forgotten', according to new NCC research

Five million working people face poverty and exclusion as they are being ignored by government and business, according to a shocking new report issued today by the National Consumer Council (NCC).

The NCC's report *More snakes than ladders?* used focus groups and interviews to get an insight into the lives of low-income workers who don't claim benefits and don't have dependent children living with them. This group, which the report calls the 'forgotten working poor', is being neglected despite making up more than a sixth of the UK's 29 million workforce.

The research reveals that while fiscal and welfare policies focus on helping families with children and pensioners, the forgotten working poor don't explicitly appear in government targets, and so are easily ignored. Everyday challenges are being made more difficult by the rising cost of basics such as food and fuel, additional charges to access or pay for essential services, as well as the credit crunch – all of which are having a disproportionate effect on the forgotten working poor, who get little help from business or the state.

'People told us about their lives and a common theme emerged – they face more obstacles than opportunities. There are five million people working hard and doing everything that society wants of them, but who are being ignored by both business and the political process,' said Nicola O'Reilly, a policy expert at the NCC.

'Politicians and service providers tend to focus mainly on helping pensioners or tackling child poverty, meaning millions of ordinary hard-working people are overlooked. Our research reveals the reality of their struggle to get by and we are calling on decision makers to take action and improve the lives of this important but neglected group.'

The research was undertaken by the Office for Public Management (OPM) for the NCC. The people asked told us that they felt:

⇨ Forgotten: The forgotten working poor feel invisible, ignored and let down by government, service providers and employers.

⇨ Skint: The rising cost of basic goods and services has a huge impact on take-home pay. The proportion of the forgotten working poor's income spent on basic essentials is growing at a faster rate than their wages. They often pay more for customer services and complaints from pay-as-you-go mobile telephones if they have no landline.

⇨ Unsettled: Limited social housing, high private rents and unafford-able home ownership leave many of the working poor living in shared accommodation, which is often temporary.

⇨ Isolated: Many people work six days a week, or take on two jobs. As a result they don't have the time to build or maintain friendships and relationships. Planning ahead is made difficult by shift rotas not being given far enough in advance and by employers restricting the planning and taking of annual leave, particularly at weekends.

⇨ Insecure: This group told us they have limited choice in the job market because of where they live, inadequate or expensive public transport, a lack of skills and barriers to re-training, which leaves many permanent workers fearing for their jobs. Being in temporary work compounds these issues – agency workers report feeling compelled to work every shift for fear of not being offered work in the future if they refused.

The NCC is proposing a number of simple solutions – ladders of opportunity – to help the millions of forgotten working poor. Recommended measures include use of a more inclusive language by policy makers such as saying 'hardworking people' not just 'hardworking families' and a review of housing policy to provide equal protection for consumers in the private and social rented sectors, more appropriate shared ownership options and more accessible, affordable rental properties.

Britain's working poor are forgotten by policy-makers

Other solutions include free customer service and complaint phone lines from local authorities, banks, insurers, telephone and pay-TV providers; more low-cost basic service options; safer and more convenient public transport services, including early and late services; and greater awareness and access to special fares. The report also calls for improved employment opportunities for low earners, through better careers advice and work-based qualifications and training that will deliver transferable skills, as well as a greater awareness of employment rights.

7 July 2008

⇨ The above information is re-printed with kind permission from the National Consumer Council. Visit www.ncc.org.uk for more information.

© National Consumer Council

Household income

Top fifth four times better off than bottom fifth

In 2006/07, original income, before taxes and benefits, of the top fifth of households in the UK was 15 times greater than that for the bottom fifth (£72,900 per household per year compared with £4,900). After redistribution through taxes and benefits, the ratio between the top and bottom fifths is reduced to four-to-one (average final income of £52,400 compared with £14,400).

Cash benefits make up 57 per cent of gross income for the poorest fifth of households, 38 per cent for the second quintile, falling to 2 per cent for the top fifth of households

Some types of household gain more than others from this redistribution. Retired households pay less in tax than they receive in benefits and so gain overall. Among non-retired households, single adult households with children also gain. Most other non-retired households pay more in tax than they receive in benefits. However, households with children do relatively better than households without children due to the cash benefits and benefits in kind (including health and education services) which are received by these households.

Cash benefits such as Income Support, Pension Credit, Child Benefit, Incapacity Benefit, and the State Retirement Pension play the largest part in reducing income inequality. They go predominantly to households with lower incomes. Cash benefits make up 57 per cent of gross income for the poorest fifth of households, 38 per cent for the

Office for National Statistics

second quintile, falling to 2 per cent for the top fifth of households.

With the exception of Council Tax and Northern Ireland rates, direct taxation is progressive; that is it takes a larger proportion of income from those households that have higher gross incomes. In 2006/07, the top fifth of households paid 25 per cent of their gross income in direct tax while the bottom fifth paid 11 per cent.

Indirect taxes are regressive, taking a higher proportion of income from those with lower incomes. Since direct and indirect taxes have opposite effects on the level of inequality, the tax system as a whole has a much smaller effect on inequality than cash benefits.

Final incomes include an adjustment for the receipt of benefits in kind from the state, such as health and education services. Households with lower incomes tend to receive more benefits in kind from the state (£7,500 for the bottom fifth compared with £3,800 for the top fifth). Retired households are the biggest users of health services provided by the state, and households with children are the biggest users of education services. Both these groups are more likely to be in lower income quintile groups.

Note: households are ranked by equivalised disposable income.
25 June 2008

⇨ The above information is reprinted with kind permission from the Office for National Statistics. Visit www.statistics.gov.uk for more.
© *Crown copyright*

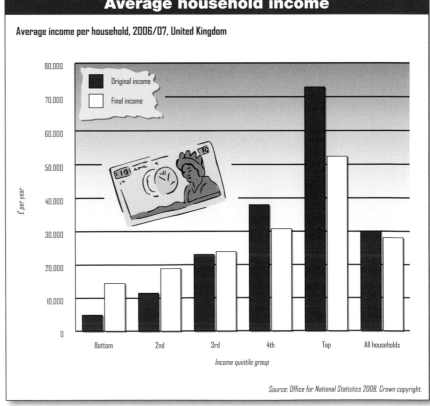

Average household income

Average income per household, 2006/07, United Kingdom

Legend: ■ Original income □ Final income

£ per year — Income quintile group

Categories: Bottom, 2nd, 3rd, 4th, Top, All households

Source: Office for National Statistics 2008. Crown copyright.

Wage gap too large, say three out of four Britons

Information from the Sutton Trust

Nearly three out of four people (74%) think that income differences in Britain are too large and seven in ten (69%) believe that parents' income plays too big a part in determining children's life chances, according to the first survey of attitudes to inequality and social mobility commissioned by the Sutton Trust.

Seven in ten (69%) believe that parents' income plays too big a part in determining children's life chances

---

The results from the Ipsos MORI survey of over 2,000 adults are consistent with academic research which has shown that background plays a bigger role in determining educational outcomes in Britain than in many other countries and that levels of social mobility are relatively low. Recent research from the Institute of Fiscal Studies meanwhile has suggested that income inequality is at its highest level since the 1960s.

The other findings of the survey paint a mixed picture of attitudes to inequality and mobility:

⇨ 69% of respondents who answered the question believed that they had experienced static or downward mobility, with the household they are in today being relatively worse off – or no better off – than the household they grew up in as a child.

⇨ Only 10% of those who answered the question and said they grew up in households in the bottom quartile of income reported being in the top quartile in adulthood.

⇨ Despite this, just 31% of respondents thought that social mobility in Britain is too low, and one-half thought it is 'about right'.

⇨ And, surprisingly, more than half (54%) agreed that people in Britain have equal opportunities to get ahead.

Dr Lee Elliot Major, Director of Research at the Sutton Trust, said: 'Opportunities in this country remain heavily determined by parental background. A wide range of research places Britain at or near the bottom of the league table of mobility, particularly in terms of the link between children's educational achievement and parental income.

'These findings suggest unease among the public about life opportunities in modern Britain, but that perceptions of mobility and inequality are mixed. The public appear to recognise some of the inequalities in our society, but on the face of it half do not think that Britain is particularly socially immobile. If we are to promote real change, a first step is to recognise that we have a problem and create a consensus on the need for reform.

'The Sutton Trust has recently brought together a range of academics, educationalists and policymakers to discuss how to promote mobility through education and to begin to build a way forward. In the Autumn we will propose a number of practical ways forward which we hope will make a real difference to people's future opportunities.'

17 July 2008

⇨ The above information is reprinted with kind permission from the Sutton Trust. Visit www.suttontrust.com for more information.

© *Sutton Trust*

Minimum living standards

Public consultation shows what people find acceptable

According to members of the public, a single person in Britain today needs to earn at least £13,400 a year before tax to afford a basic but acceptable standard of living. This 'minimum income standard', based on the extensive deliberations of ordinary people supported by experts, shows the cost of covering basic goods and services for different household types.

A minimum income standard for Britain: What people think, published today (1 July), by the Joseph Rowntree Foundation, captures the consensus reached among ordinary people (on a range of incomes) about what they feel is needed to achieve an acceptable standard of living today. Thirty-nine groups from different kinds of household (such as families with children, pensioners and single people) had detailed discussions about the necessary elements of a household budget for each family type. Experts looked at these budgets to ensure that they provided an adequate diet and met basic needs like keeping a home warm.

Participants in this study were clear that a minimum living standard should provide for more than mere survival. One older woman taking part in the research summed up this view: 'Food and shelter keeps you alive, it doesn't make you live.' Findings from this extensive consultation with members of the public showed that:

⇨ A single person without children needs to spend £158 a week, and a couple with two children £370 a week, not including rent or mortgage.

⇨ To afford this budget on top of rent on a modest council home, the single person would need to earn £13,400 a year before tax and the couple with two children £26,800.

⇨ For families with no adult working, state benefits provide for less than half the minimum budget for single people and around two-thirds for those with children. The basic state pension provides a retired couple with about three-quarters of the minimum, but if they claim the means-tested Pension Credit their income is topped up to just above the minimum income standard.

⇨ The minimum income is above the official 'poverty line' of 60% median income, for nearly all household groups. This shows that almost everybody classified as being in poverty has income too low to pay for a standard of living regarded as 'adequate' by all members of the public who took part in this research.

A single person without children needs to spend £158 a week to achieve a minimum living standard

---

Julia Unwin, Director of the Joseph Rowntree Foundation, said: 'This research is designed to encourage debate, and to start building a public consensus about what level of income no one should have to live below. Of course, everyone has their own views about what items in a family budget are "essential". But this is the best effort to date to enable ordinary people to discuss and agree what all households should be able to afford.

'Naturally, people's circumstances and preferences vary, and this research does not dictate how people should spend their money. But it does start to pin down how much people think is needed to be able to afford basic opportunities and choices that allow proper participation in society.'

Co-author Jonathan Bradshaw, Professor of Social Policy at the University of York, said: 'Until now, poverty assessments have been largely based on rather arbitrary measures of relative income, which are helpful for monitoring trends but leave unanswered the question of how much income is enough. Based on these public assessments, almost everyone defined as living below the official poverty line falls short of what people judge to be adequate for their fellow citizens – sometimes by quite a long way.'

Co-author Noel Smith, from the Centre for Research in Social Policy at Loughborough University, said: 'This study has allowed us to engage in detailed and productive discussions with people from all walks of life about what anyone should be able to afford. These groups have taken their task very seriously, in lively and thoughtful discussions about all aspects of a household's spending. This is not about what ordinary people would like to have, but about what they consider to be basic needs.'

Notes

1 The full report, *A minimum income standard for Britain: What people think*, by Jonathan Bradshaw, Sue Middleton, Abigail Davis, Nina Oldfield, Noel Smith, Linda Cusworth and Julie Williams is published by the Joseph Rowntree Foundation. More information is available at www.minimumincomestandard.org

2 The whole consultation process with members of the public was based on the following definition which was agreed by an initial set of groups: 'A minimum standard of living in Britain today includes, but is more than just, food, clothes and shelter. It is about having what you need in order to have the opportunities and choices necessary to participate in society.'
1 July 2008

⇨ The above press release is reprinted with kind permission from the Joseph Rowntree Foundation. Visit www.jrf.org.uk for more information.

© Joseph Rowntree Foundation

Growing inequality

Do people know and do they care?

Private equity player and Gordon Brown confidant Sir Ronald Cohen said recently that the gap between the 'haves' and the 'have-nots' could lead to street riots if nothing is done to reduce it. But do ordinary people care? And if not, why not?

A new study by the Institute for Social and Economic Research sheds light on the apparent quiescence of the British public in the face of growing inequality. In a recent series of detailed interviews and focus groups, Professor Ray Pahl and his colleagues find that:

⇨ People have much higher material expectations nowadays: what might have been aspirational in the 1960s is considered a basic necessity today. This affluence seems to have produced a relative contentment.

⇨ While people may have some sense of a large disparity between top earners and people 'at the bottom', they are not necessarily well informed about particular occupational incomes.

⇨ Nor are people likely to be aware of incomes, even among those known to them personally – their siblings, friends and neighbours. With dual earner households, it seems even more unlikely that people know with any accuracy exactly how much money other households have.

⇨ When asked whether they compare themselves with people outside their immediate social contexts, people refer both up and down the social scale: to the super rich, whose fabulous lifestyles are featured on TV and in magazines; and to people at 'the bottom' of society whom they strongly resent – people on benefits, shirkers, refugees and asylum-seekers.

⇨ When people make social comparisons, they explicitly refer to differences in terms of lifestyle – to the visible trappings of consumerism, such as the kind of house and area in which people live, the car they drive and the clothes they wear. Of these, houses and neighbourhoods are seen as the strongest indicators of how well people are doing.

⇨ There is little evidence of sentiments of solidarity: the notion of fraternalism seems to have largely receded from contemporary discourse. Instead people speak overwhelmingly in terms of *individual* career trajectories, *individual* lifestyle and consumption choices and an *individual* assessment of their social position in relation to other individuals.

Professor Ray Pahl comments on the findings:

'The focus on the individual may be, in part, a product of a subtle shift in political rhetoric, particularly in the Labour Party, rebranding Britain as a "market" rather than as a "capitalist" society, in which individual consumers are encouraged to make choices between both public and private goods and services, even when such "choice" is in practice non-existent or illusory.

'Our exploration of the overall theme of social comparisons finds little evidence of the articulation of serious resentment. We thus tend to agree with J.K. Galbraith that *The Affluent Society* has led to *The Culture of Contentment* as the titles of his books put it.'

People have much higher material expectations nowadays

'Such a conclusion may be reassuring to politicians anxious to co-opt the "middle mass" into managerialist policies. But it might be unwise to be too complacent: the middle mass may consume individually and have similar lifestyle aspirations, but they are collectively and seriously in debt. Capitalism could return to bite.'

Source: ISER (Sept. 2007) 'Growing Inequality: Do people know and do they care?', ISER Press Release 2007-16, refers to Pahl, R; Rose, D. and Spencer, L. (2007) 'Inequality and quiescence: a continuing conundrum', ISER Working Paper, No. 2007-22. Colchester: University of Essex.
24 September 2007

⇨ The above information is reprinted with kind permission from the Institute for Social and Economic Research. Visit www.iser.essex.ac.uk for more information.

© *University of Essex*

- THE CAR, THE HOUSE THE ENTERTAINMENT SYSTEM...

ER... IT'S CAPITALISM ON THE PHONE... ABOUT THE DEBT...

Disabled people and poverty

Report exposes millions of disabled people trapped in poverty

Millions of disabled people across the UK are trapped in poverty, reveals a major report out today (January 8, 2008).

The Leonard Cheshire Disability report, *Disability Poverty in the UK*, shows that disabled people are twice as likely to live in poverty as non-disabled people.

They are also more likely to live in poverty today than they were 10 years ago. There are an estimated three million disabled people living in relative poverty in the UK .

Yet, on average, disabled people's day-to-day living costs – for basics like mobility aids, care and transport – are a quarter (25 per cent) higher than those of non-disabled people.

Disability Poverty in the UK calls on the government to urgently develop a strategy to end disability poverty, exposing the missing link in the government's overall strategy to tackle children's and older people's poverty.

It is released just a day after senior Labour backbench MP Roger Berry tabled a Parliamentary motion, which already has cross-party support, calling on the government to take action to tackle disability poverty.

It is the first time a report has defined and quantified the full extent of disability poverty in the UK – way beyond just finance and income.

The report sets out a number of recommendations on issues, ranging from savings to housing, to help bring about change. It also outlines a series of 'indicators' to monitor all aspects of disability poverty, from income to quality of life.

'Disability poverty is one of the most significant, and most challenging, problems facing the UK today,' says report author Guy Parckar, Public Policy Manager at Leonard Cheshire Disability.

'The failure to specifically tackle disability poverty represents a gaping hole in the government's otherwise strong record on poverty. Our report sets out a route for the government to begin to tackle this massively important issue and start the work to end disability poverty.'

Roger Berry MP said: 'It is clear from Leonard Cheshire Disability's report that disability poverty has been missing from the political agenda for too long. The levels of disability poverty in the UK today are unacceptable.

Disabled people are twice as likely to live in poverty as non-disabled people

---

'This report is an urgent and important challenge to the government – action is needed now to ensure millions of disabled people are not condemned to a life in inescapable poverty.'

Disability Poverty in the UK paints a picture of how poverty can impact on many areas of a disabled person's life. For example:

➩ Continuing low levels of employment for disabled people mean that many are trapped in inescapable poverty. For people not expected to work, benefit levels frequently fail to cover basic costs of living, leaving them with no real route out of poverty.

➩ Half (49 per cent) of disabled people surveyed by Leonard Cheshire Disability had no savings. The majority revealed this was because their incomes were way below the national average.

➩ Disabled people face major discrimination in the education system. For example, disabled people are more than twice as likely to have no qualifications as non-disabled people.

The Leonard Cheshire Disability report makes a significant number of recommendations to help end disability poverty. This includes extending Winter Fuel Allowance to many disabled people who would also benefit from support with heating costs and reviewing how disability benefits support those disabled people who are not expected to work.

8 January 2008

➩ The above information is re-printed with kind permission from Leonard Cheshire Disability. Visit www.lcdisability.org for more.

© *Leonard Cheshire Disability*

Paying the price of poverty

Child poverty is costing UK taxpayers more than £40 billion a year

The consequences of allowing it to continue – crime, ill health and low employment – are expensive, as US research shows.

Now children's charity Barnardo's is calling for the huge cost of child poverty in the UK to be calculated properly, with the backing of the American academic behind the revelation, Professor Harry Holzer.

In a simplistic translation from the calculations made in the US, Barnardo's estimates that the costs to the UK economy in not tackling child poverty total more than £40 billion a year.

Barnardo's Chief Executive and Chair of the Campaign to End Child Poverty Martin Narey said: 'The primary reason we want to end child poverty is a moral one, but there is also an economic case for eliminating it. Research in the US shows that the failure to tackle child poverty there, in additional health and criminal justice costs and in reduced tax revenues amounts to 3.8% of American GDP or $500 billion every year.

'We are calling on the Government to set up a UK Commission on Child Poverty to set out the policies and investment needed to hit the Government targets to halve child poverty by 2010 and eradicate it by 2020.

'Poverty does not just affect the 3.8 million children who are living below the breadline today – it affects everyone both socially and financially.

It is shameful and damaging to us all, that the fourth or fifth richest country in the world allows one in three of its children to live in poverty.'

Prof Holzer, Professor of Public Policy at Georgetown University and visiting fellow at the Urban Institute, Washington DC, said: 'When children grow up in poverty they are more likely than those who aren't poor to have low earnings as adults, which in turn reflects lower workforce productivity.

'A minority are more likely to engage in crime which imposes large monetary costs on their victims, as well as the criminal justice system.

'Poor children are also more likely to suffer from ill health throughout life. As adults their poor health generates illness and early mortality which not only requires large healthcare expenditure, but also creates a direct loss of goods and services that they could be generating should they be fit to work.'

Executive director of the Task Force on Poverty for the Center for American Progress Mark Greenberg has put together a strategy to halve child poverty in the US, based on a British model, called From Poverty To Prosperity.

He will appear alongside Prof Holzer at a seminar – hosted by Barnardo's and attended by Secretary of State for Work and Pensions Peter Hain – called Paying The Price Of Child Poverty, on Monday.

Mr Greenberg said: 'To reach the public it is important to combine a moral case with an economic case. It is wrong for children to grow up in poverty, but the continuation of child poverty also hurts all of us, by imposing costs on the economy as a whole.

'Cutting child poverty does require new expenditures, but these costs are not as great as the ongoing losses to the economy by allowing it to continue.'

Harry Holzer and Mark Greenberg are due to speak at Paying The Price of Child Poverty, along with Donald Hirsch, Special Adviser, Joseph Rowntree Foundation, and Richard Wilkinson, Professor of Social Epidemiology, Nottingham University.

It will be held at Central Hall, Storey's Gate, Westminster, on October 29, between 10am and 1.30pm.

Paying The Price Of Child Poverty is part of Barnardo's campaign to keep the Government to its promise to halve the number of children living in poverty by 2010 and eradicate childhood poverty by 2020.
29 October 2007

⇨ The above information is reprinted with kind permission from Barnardo's. Visit www.barnardos.org.uk for more information.
© Barnardo's 2008

Poverty and debt

Poverty forces families into high-cost loans to provide for their children

A new report by Save the Children reveals that as many as 2.3 million people in the UK on low incomes are being forced to take out high-interest loans at rates topping 183% APR – many simply to provide essentials for their children.

Save the Children's report *Robbing Peter to Pay Paul* shows how desperate parents have to choose between essentials for themselves or adequate clothing, meals and heating for their children.

It also reveals how easy it is for parents struggling to provide the basics for their children to be forced into taking out loans at exorbitant rates of interest, which in turn can drag families down into the quicksand of unpayable debt.

Report author Jason Strelitz, Save the Children's UK poverty advisor, says that millions of people resort to high-cost credit. Typical examples include companies such as Provident, known as a 'doorstep lender' because it provides credit and collects repayments door-to-door, or Brighthouse, which targets deprived areas of the UK selling household goods on credit at extremely high rates.

As many as 2.3 million people in the UK on low incomes are being forced to take out high-interest loans at rates topping 183% APR – many simply to provide essentials for their children

---

According to Mr Strelitz one of the problems is that many poor people are unable to obtain credit from banks and cheaper lenders, often because they are considered too high a risk.

'Doorstep lenders exploit poor families' inability to get credit from more mainstream lenders and they cover their risk in lending to the less well off by charging punitive interest rates.'

'The core problem is not the companies themselves, but the poverty that forces people to use them,' says Mr Strelitz.

Rather than calling for these companies to be further regulated – which could risk leaving families with no credit options at all, or driving people into the arms of loan sharks – Save the Children sees this as a call to action on eradicating child poverty.

'This is about tackling symptoms, not causes,' says Mr Strelitz. 'The government is off track in meeting its own target of halving child poverty by 2010.'

Save the Children, as a member of the Campaign to End Child Poverty, is asking the government to invest £4 billion to support the incomes of the poorest families in UK.

Also, Save the Children is campaigning for the introduction of seasonal grants of £100 per child living in poverty to be paid in summer and winter – the most financially demanding times of the year for poor families.

'We have found that there are two times in the year when families are most likely to need extra cash – during the summer holidays when children are off school and need extra meals, and at Christmas when the heating has to be on all day.'

These grants could lift up to 440,000 children out of poverty.

Save the Children also believes there is a greater role for mainstream banks and voluntary sector lenders such as credit unions to provide affordable and appropriate credit for low income families.

10 December 2007

⇨ The above information is reprinted with kind permission from Save the Children. Visit www.savethechildren.org.uk for more information.

Living with hardship 24/7

The diverse experiences of families in poverty in England

This ground-breaking report from the Frank Buttle Trust, University of York and the NSPCC looked in depth at the experience of families living on a low income in both affluent and deprived neighbourhoods. Families who participated came from a range of ethnic backgrounds. They were contacted through Children's Services, voluntary organisations and schools. Based on interviews with parents, children (aged five-11) and professionals, the findings highlight the need for more recognition of the many ways in which poverty impacts on families' lives and for a holistic approach to supporting parents and children. The bulleted points below are key findings.

⇨ Many experiences of hardship were common across different contexts. There were also important differences in the challenges families faced. Families in deprived areas had worse housing conditions and greater worries about crime and unsafe neighbourhoods, and some children experienced the stress of a more violent local culture within the community and/or at school. Families in affluent areas had less access to affordable activities for children and other amenities, and children's experiences of bullying were often clearly related to poverty.

⇨ The challenges for families living on a low income were aggravated by experiences of abuse, domestic violence, relationship breakdown, bereavement, mental health problems, bullying and feeling unsafe. Some life experiences made poverty more difficult to manage and poverty made all other forms of adversity more difficult to cope with.

⇨ Children as young as five reported a range of worries, including some very serious concerns about their families' circumstances.

Children were keenly aware of the difficulties their parents faced, and some responded by hiding their own needs and worries from their parents. Poverty impacted in a range of ways on all dimensions of children's well-being.

⇨ Conflict within the home, siblings with behaviour problems, difficult relationships with non-resident parents and bullying were key sources of unhappiness for children. Disputes over contact with non-resident parents were very stressful for children and children's views had sometimes been overridden by the courts.

⇨ Grandparents were important sources of support and played a key role in mitigating hardship for parents and children. Nearly half the children had no grandparents in their social networks, however – the availability and involvement of grandparents was restricted mainly by past maltreatment of the parents (often resulting in estrangement) or immigration.

⇨ Parents' wider support networks were also affected by poverty and other adverse life experiences, such as abuse and domestic violence. Men and those who immigrated as adults had smaller support networks.

⇨ Behavioural problems among children were common, especially but not only among boys. Poverty, poor/overcrowded housing and lack of resources for therapy or counselling, respite care and/or activities for children all exacerbated these problems.

Parents had often found it difficult to access help with these issues and, for most, what support they received came too late.

The experience of poverty today – commonalities and diversities

For the families in this study, poverty meant going without what the vast majority of people in the UK take for granted. Their lives were significantly restricted by poverty. Many could not afford basics such as a cooked meal each day for adults or toys for children. Constant prioritising and juggling were required – 'robbing Peter to pay Paul' as some put it. In this context, the smallest things, such as deodorant or moisturiser, could become luxuries that had to be saved up for. Poverty was often self-perpetuating – for example, where poorly insulated housing meant increased heating bills. Many went into debt to get essential items such as clothes or to pay utility bills. Dealing with agencies over benefits and tax credits was demanding and stressful. Fluctuations of income, as a result of mistakes or reassessments, were very difficult to manage.

Although tax credits were helpful, paid work was still not worth it for many parents, and those who worked were sometimes worse off for doing so. Many of those without paid work would have preferred to be working. Barriers to work included the costs and availability of childcare, the structure and inflexibility of the benefit system, lack of skills or experience, lack of jobs at sufficient pay to make it worth working, immigration status, parents' own or their partners' health problems and a range of concerns about children.

Common psychological impacts of poverty were that families felt trapped by lack of options, felt guilty about being unable to meet their own and their children's expectations, and had difficulty planning ahead when living in unpredictable circumstances.

While these were experiences common across most families, there were also ways in which the experience of hardship varied, and was influenced by gender, ethnicity and class and whether the family lived in an affluent or a deprived neighbourhood. Families in deprived areas had worse housing conditions and greater fears about crime and unsafe neighbourhoods than those in more affluent areas. Families in affluent areas had less access to affordable activities for children and other amenities. Children in affluent areas were more aware of their relative poverty. Parents from middle-class backgrounds who had fallen into poverty often had high aspirations for their children, but their sense of being different from those around them could inhibit their own and their children's relationships with other local families and their use of local resources.

Stigma was widespread and contributed to families' isolation. It was associated with poverty particularly for families living in more affluent areas. Stigma and feelings of low social value were also experienced by families affected by domestic violence, by disabilities or with mental health problems. It was particularly intense for women in the Bangladeshi community:

'I feel people look at us differently to other friends/family – they feel sorry for us and say not to buy presents or bring food for social gatherings or family events. Their pity makes me feel low. At times we avoid these situations.' (Bangladeshi woman)

Hooper, CA., Gorin, S., Cabral, C. & Dyson, C. (2007) Living with hardship 24/7: the diverse experiences of families in poverty in England. The Frank Buttle Trust, London.

November 2007

⇨ This summary is based on a research project developed by the Frank Buttle Trust, the NSPCC and the University of York, working in partnership. The research project was funded by the Big Lottery Fund. Reprinted with kind permission from the Frank Buttle Trust. Visit www.buttletrust.org for more.

© Frank Buttle Trust

Public attitudes to child poverty

Information from the Department for Work and Pensions

Findings are published today from a survey commissioned by the Department for Work and Pensions (DWP) looking at public attitudes to child poverty. DWP placed the survey questions on a national face-to-face omnibus survey of 1,500 members of the public, which was carried out by an independent research organisation in July-September 2007. Key findings from the survey show that:

⇨ Forty-one per cent of respondents thought there was very little real child poverty in Britain today; 53 per cent thought there was quite a lot.

⇨ Most respondents thought that child poverty in Britain had increased or stayed the same over the last decade, and most thought it would increase or stay the same over the next ten years.

⇨ Just over half (57 per cent) of respondents thought an unemployed single mother living solely on state benefits would be hard up or really poor. This figure fell slightly, to 52 per cent, when respondents were given the amount they might commonly receive (£123 per week after housing and council tax costs).

⇨ Over two-thirds (69 per cent) of respondents thought that a couple family with two children living solely on income from the father's full-time work on the minimum wage, with tax credits, would be hard up or really poor. This figure fell to 49 per cent when respondents were given an example amount they might receive (£241 per week after housing and council tax costs).

⇨ Eighty per cent of respondents thought central government had responsibility for addressing child poverty. Local government was chosen by a third (35 per cent). Individuals/families were also chosen by a third (again, 35 per cent).[1]

⇨ Respondents were asked to select three reasons they thought best explained child poverty from a list of thirteen. The three most frequently chosen reasons were:
  ↪ their parents suffer from alcoholism, drug abuse or other addictions (45 per cent);[2]
  ↪ there has been a family break-up or loss of a family member (38 per cent); and,
  ↪ their parents' work doesn't pay enough (37 per cent).

Notes

1 Respondents could choose more than one option.

2 Evidence suggests that 4 per cent of lone parents have alcohol dependence and 2 per cent drug dependence. The respective figures for couples with children are 3 per cent and 1 per cent. Ref: Gould N (2006) *Mental health and child poverty*, York: Joseph Rowntree Foundation.

20 March 2008

⇨ The above information is reprinted with kind permission from the Department for Work and Pensions. Visit www.dwp.gov.uk for more.

© Crown copyright

Keeping mum

Mother's low income the source of 70% of child poverty

Today (12th May 2008), leading women's rights organisation the Fawcett Society launches a new campaign, Keeping Mum, exposing the links between women's poverty and child poverty. The campaign is being run in partnership with Unite the Union and Oxfam.

Fawcett has obtained previously unpublished statistics which reveal the extent to which child poverty is caused by the gender income gap and the lack of opportunities for mothers in the labour market.

The figures show that:

⇨ Four out of ten (39%) of children in poverty are in single-mother households.

⇨ A further three out of ten (29%) are in households where the father works full-time, but the mother is on low income or no income.

⇨ In addition, the statistics show that lone mothers are at double the risk of being in poverty as couples with children.

From the moment they conceive a child, women face immediate financial penalties:

⇨ Mothers are at greater risk of poverty in the UK than in any other western European country.

⇨ 30,000 women every year lose their jobs as a result of becoming pregnant.

⇨ After having a child, many more women move into low-paid and insecure work as cleaners, carers, temps and homeworkers, which does not keep them above the poverty line.

The Fawcett Society is calling on the government to tackle mothers' poverty by:

⇨ Banning the dismissal of pregnant women.

⇨ Increasing maternity and paternity entitlements to the same level as the minimum wage.

⇨ Making gender pay audits compulsory for all organisations.

⇨ Increasing the number of hours mothers can work without losing their benefits from four to sixteen.

⇨ Introducing measures to encourage fathers to be more involved in children's upbringing.

Commenting on the campaign, Dr Katherine Rake, Director of the Fawcett Society, said:

'Having a baby in the UK puts women at risk of moving into poverty. This means that child poverty and mothers' poverty have common causes and common solutions.

'We will only succeed in ending child poverty when we address mothers' inequality by ensuring they have access to equal pay, adequate benefits and freedom from discrimination.

'The time has come for the government to stop keeping mum about the links between women's inequality and children's poverty, and to start taking action to support mums.'

Cath Speight, National Political Officer of Unite the Union, commented:

'Unite is pleased to be supporting this important campaign. The welfare of children cannot be separated from that of their mothers and it is not acceptable that women and children are living in poverty in this country. Women have waited long enough for equal pay – urgent action is now required if the Government is to achieve their target of eradicating child poverty.'

Kate Wareing, Director for UK Poverty at Oxfam, commented:

'At Oxfam, our experience teaches us that poverty is caused by circumstances beyond an individual's control. Child poverty will not be ended if we do not tackle the root causes of why women – particularly mothers – are poorer than men. Ending child poverty requires us to raise the income of low-paid women, end discrimination against pregnant women and mothers at work and close the gender pay gap.'

39% of children in poverty are in single-mother households

Kate Green, Director of Child Poverty Action Group, commented:

'Nearly a third of British children live below the poverty line. Poor pay, lack of flexible working and employer discrimination leave mothers unable to access employment and at higher risk of poverty, whether as part of a couple or a lone parent. At the same time, lone mothers with important reasons to stay at home caring for their child are mostly left languishing below the poverty line by an inadequate safety net. Ending inequality for mothers is an important part of ending Britain's child poverty shame.'

TUC General Secretary Brendan Barber commented:

'This report shows how the whole family suffers when women are under-paid and their work is under-valued. The Government cannot hope to meet its commitment of ending child poverty unless serious inroads are made into closing both the full-time and part-time gender pay gaps.'
12 May 2008

⇨ Information from the Fawcett Society. Visit www.fawcettsociety. org.uk for more information.

© *Fawcett Society*

The cost of education

Three out of four parents find school costs difficult to meet

Three out of four parents and guardians find meeting their child's school costs 'very' or 'quite' difficult, according to a new survey from national charity Citizens Advice. Costs can be high and include many items during the year, such as uniform, books, school trips, photos. Nearly half of all respondents were asked to contribute to school funds, with some reporting they were pressured to make 'voluntary' contributions.

Nearly one in ten respondents indicated that the costs associated with schooling had actually affected their choice of school. The results come from an online survey conducted by national charity Citizens Advice of more than 1,000 people during June and July 2007 on its website (www.adviceguide.org.uk).

Parents continue to say that uniform is still a big expense, despite Government guidelines calling for schools to make uniform more affordable.

The majority of respondents (59%) said they expect to have to pay more for uniform from September this year than they did last year.

One lone parent who completed the survey said her daughter's secondary school uniform would cost her an entire week's wage.

Two in five respondents said there was no financial help available to them, whilst one in four respondents were unaware of any help. Less than 7% said there were local authority grants available.

The cost of uniforms varies enormously, with some parents reporting spending as much as £500 per year. A third of primary school respondents spent more than £150 on school uniform and PE kit per year. Half of all secondary school respondents spent more than £200 per year.

David Harker, Chief Executive for Citizens Advice, said,

'Parents shouldn't have to spend sleepless nights worrying about how they are going to pay for what their child needs simply to go to school. For many it doesn't feel like a "free" education, it is hitting their budgets very hard and potentially having a direct impact on children's schooling. I am especially concerned about schools that put pressure on parents to make so-called "voluntary" contributions.

One lone parent who completed the survey said her daughter's secondary school uniform would cost her an entire week's wage

---

'The Government should take stronger action against schools to make uniform policies more realistic and affordable and should monitor schools to make sure they stick to the guidelines. It would also really help if all local authorities in England were required to provide uniform grants for families which receive the maximum child tax credit.

'We want to help parents feel they can complain about school costs and how much notice schools give for expenses. Parent power can help put pressure on schools to make education affordable for everyone.'

School trips and other expenses

Nearly half of all respondents said they had been asked to contribute to school funds. Nearly all had been asked to pay for photographs, with six out of ten respondents being asked to contribute to equipment for lessons, such as cooking equipment and arts and crafts materials. The majority (63%) had been asked to contribute to fundraising activities and school parties and discos.

For day trips, more than half of respondents said they paid more than £10 for a day trip, with nearly half of those paying up to £15. 3% of respondents paid more than £50 on day trips. For residential trips, one in five respondents said they paid more than £200, with nearly 3% paying more than £500.

Nearly half (43%) of all respondents said they did not think that they were given sufficient notice to budget for day trips, with one in five (22%) saying they did not feel they were given sufficient notice for residential trips.

Four out of five respondents (78%) said that it was not clear that families on a low income could be exempt from some or all of the cost of the trips.

Citizens Advice is a member of the School Costs Coalition which includes Barnardo's, Child Poverty Action Group, End Child Poverty, Family Welfare Association, One Parent Families, NUT and Save the Children.

The Horizons project for lone parents, supported by Barclaycard, funds grants for uniform and other costs through the charity the Family Welfare Association (FWA). The FWA gave out almost £200,000 in school uniform grants in the financial year 2006/07 which benefited more then 2,500 children.

Comments from parents and guardians as part of the survey

'I am a single parent. My youngest child is starting secondary school in September...It is compulsory to have everything with the embroidered school logo on purchased at a specific shop. The cost is really high compared to the supermarket...her uniform will cost me just over one week's wage'
Citizens Advice survey respondent, Wigan

'My son was disciplined in front of the whole class because he had the wrong trousers on and I could not afford to buy new ones, he had gone through the knee on his old pair'
Citizens Advice survey respondent, Essex, primary school

'I could buy two polo shirts in town for £5 but it costs £9 for one from the school as it has the school name on it and you have to have the name.'

Citizens Advice survey respondent, East Sussex, secondary school

'I find it really frustrating that uniform shirts and jumpers are only available from specific shops, and are very expensive, but appalling quality, therefore forcing parents to buy at least twice in the school year to replace uniform that has fallen to bits!'
Wales: Isle of Anglesey, secondary school

'My daughter's uniform for starting high school costs over £500, we got a £12 grant. What a joke'
Citizens Advice survey respondent, Sefton, secondary school

'My children don't go on many school trips due to the cost most times I keep them off school on the day of trips so they don't get picked on.'
Citizens Advice survey respondent, City of Peterborough, secondary school

'The thing I was really angry about was to be told that my daughter wouldn't be able to take home a piece of her work at the end of the year unless you paid a voluntary contribution...I FELT BLACKMAILED...it's important for them to feel proud by bringing home their work to show you' (emphasis in original)
East Sussex, secondary school

'I think the school my children go to is great however they have a voluntary payment – school fund which they send you reminder letters if you don't pay it, even though it is voluntary'
Worcestershire, primary school
29 August 2007

⇨ The above information is reprinted with kind permission from the Citizens Advice Bureau. Visit www.citizensadvice.org.uk for more information.

© *Citizens Advice Bureau*

Social exclusion and education

Young children see poverty holding them back at school

Children in poverty face greatly reduced educational prospects and future life chances. This is the conclusion not just of social policy experts and government statisticians, but of young children themselves. Emerging research published by the Joseph Rowntree Foundation (JRF) shows that children are aware of such outcomes from an early age and that their own stereotyping reinforces these differences.

Eight reports looking into the experiences and attitudes of children from different backgrounds represent the first phase of a major new JRF programme on education and poverty.

Social background influences the way children feel about school from an early age. At primary school, children in poverty are more likely to have negative experiences and feel 'got at' by teachers. Donald Hirsch, author of the *Round-up* summary of the work, said, 'This doesn't necessarily mean

JOSEPH ROWNTREE FOUNDATION

teachers are prejudiced, but that low-income children find themselves in schools where the pressures are greater, and this reinforces prior disadvantages.'

While children from all backgrounds see the advantages of school, deprived children are more likely to feel anxious and unconfident about school. Out-of-school activities can help build self-confidence by improving learning relationships, and children from advantaged backgrounds greatly benefit from the access they have to more structured and supervised activities beyond school.

A crucial difference highlighted by the research is in experiences of homework. Children from poorer families are less likely to have space in which to do their homework, or to get as much help from parents as children with higher socio-economic status. Poorer parents may be under greater pressure. They may also lack the confidence in their own abilities and have bad memories of school.

Children in poverty face greatly reduced educational prospects and future life chances

'Poorer children do less well not just because their parents read to them less, but because of the rest of their life experience. If we are serious about improving the life chances of the poorest children, we have to do much more than worry about the curriculum,' added Hirsch.

The research also found that many children and young people who become disaffected with school develop strong resentments about mistreatment (including perceptions of racial discrimination) and these issues need to be taken into account when working with such children. Work with disaffected young people is most effective where it creates a new environment and new relationships, where children feel more involved in their own futures.

Only a quarter of students receiving free school meals gain five good GCSEs or equivalent, compared to over half the overall population in England. The gap between the outcomes of children from disadvantaged backgrounds and those from advantaged backgrounds is wider in the UK than in most other similar countries. Hirsch concluded, 'We're not talking about just a small group of children in "extreme circumstances". The issues highlighted in this research affect one in four of our children.'
7 September 2007

⇨ The above press release is reprinted with kind permission from the Joseph Rowntree Foundation. Visit www.jrf.org.uk for more information.
© Joseph Rowntree Foundation

2 skint 4 school

Information from the Child Poverty Action Group

What does child poverty have to do with educational achievement?

The Government has implemented wide-ranging educational reforms and per-pupil spending levels are now up to 'record levels'. And yet the attainment gap between rich and poor pupils gets wider as they progress through the education system.

⇨ By 3 years old, poor children may be up to a year behind the wealthiest children in terms of cognitive development and 'school readiness'.

⇨ Wealthier pupils perform better at all stages of schooling than pupils eligible for free school meals, regardless of race or gender.

⇨ By the time they move to secondary school poorer children are on average two years behind better-off children.

High performing pupils at primary school are four times more likely to fall into low achievement by GCSEs if they are poor

⇨ High performing pupils at primary school are four times more likely to fall into low achievement by GCSEs if they are poor.

⇨ Being poor means a pupil is nearly three times as likely to fail to get at least five A-C grades at GCSE – and the grade gap with the wealthiest pupils is widening.

⇨ Just over 6% of poor pupils receiving free school meals remain at school to take A levels, compared to around 40% of students overall.

⇨ 60,000 state school pupils in the top 20% of academic performers do not go on to higher education each year.

What problems do children from poor families face?

Children do not leave the problems of social and economic inequality behind at the school gates – they carry them into the classroom:

⇨ Poor children are more likely to have health problems from birth, and to develop disabilities and special educational needs.

⇨ Families with low incomes and bad housing struggle to provide a strong learning environment at home.

⇨ A child who is stressed, hungry and stigmatised is unlikely to thrive in the classroom.

A 2003 government study found:

⇨ Parents of secondary pupils spend on average around £1,000 on extra school costs like uniforms, trips and equipment.

⇨ 55% of low income families find it difficult to meet extra school costs.

⇨ Pupils whose parents can't afford the cost of an activity or trip are twice as likely to pretend they do not want to do it as to tell the school they cannot afford it.

A 2007 survey of more than 1,000 parents by the School Costs Coalition found:

⇨ Over 10% said extra school costs affected their choice of school.

Why aren't things getting better?

Policy makers and political parties are focusing on the wrong areas: on endless reforms of school management structures, disciplinary ethos and ownership of schools. Core problems not being addressed include:

⇨ Schools are failing to target additional resources on the children who need it most.

⇨ Parental choice is favouring wealthier parents and generating educational inequalities.

⇨ Local authorities have more demands heaped on them, yet do not have the resources or the power to redistribute wealth to poorer families.

⇨ Less attention is focused on tackling the causes of poverty – by raising family income – than on dealing with its consequences in the classroom.

⇨ The Government is not recognising the extent to which child poverty drives educational failure and that improvements require more support for poor families.

What needs to change?

Lack of family income is damaging children's educational outcomes and making teachers' jobs much harder. Families need more money to ensure their children are well fed, warm, live in safe and secure environments and can participate in the full range of cultural and social activities outside of school. The Government must ensure all children access all parts of the education system. Reducing poverty and improving child well-being must be placed at the heart of the Government's educational agenda. Reducing child poverty and its impact through action in the following areas will reduce the educational attainment gap:

Family incomes for education

Children do not leave social and economic inequality at the school gates – they bring them into the classroom. Being poor harms their well-being and limits their ability to learn. Poorer children are more likely to be tired, hungry and disengaged from the educational process. They often can't afford to participate in social, sporting or creative activities in the wider community. The most effective way of targeting additional funds on disadvantaged children is to make sure families receive the money they need to keep their children out of poverty and to support their education.

Homes fit for learning

A cold, cramped home without a quiet warm place to study, without equipment like books or computers, damages children's lives and educational experiences. Constant moves and temporary accommodation generate insecurity and stress. Homes fit for learning – and living – must be placed at the heart of the educational agenda.

Genuinely free education

Schools' charging policies mean that a 'free' education can cost hundreds of pounds per child. Poor families may have to pay for school trips, music lessons or revision guides. Poor children in working families may not be entitled to free school meals. Poor children in non-working families may be excluded from childcare and extended school provision because their parents do not qualify for the childcare element of working tax credit. This damages child wellbeing, compromises teachers and compounds educational inequalities. The Government must ensure that all children access all aspects of the educational system; and schools must ensure children are not stigmatised or excluded from any school-based activities.

Support for teachers

The most committed teacher cannot compensate the poorest children for the ill health, poor housing, and lack of opportunities that blight their lives. The Government must address the causes of poverty and teachers need more support to help them cope with its consequences. Schools – and teacher training courses – must ensure that teachers have the skills, training and specialist support they need to cope with the diverse challenges associated with child poverty.

Good schools for all

Selection – and parental 'choice' – exclude poor children from 'good' schools. This may damage children's educational experiences and aspirations in 'disadvantaged' schools. In the classroom, poor children's needs may be sacrificed to the demands of league tables or parental choice. The Government must recognise that some of its policies are generating educational inequality, and others are proving ineffective. It must do more to ensure that all schools get the best out of all the children in their care. Reducing educational charges and providing universal free school meals will help make all schools more accessible learning environments.

⇨ The above information is reprinted with kind permission from the Child Poverty Action Group. Visit www.cpag.org.uk for more information.

© *Child Poverty Action Group*

Child poverty: true or false?

Information from Save the Children

'*3.8 million children in the UK live in poverty.*'
TRUE. 3.8 million children means more than one in every four children in the UK.
'*Some parents in the UK only have £19 a day to cover electricity, gas, phones, other bills, food, clothes, washing, transport, health needs and activities.*'
TRUE.
'*Most poor families own a car.*'
FALSE. Most poor families do not own a car.
'*About 7,700 children in the UK can't afford a healthy diet.*'
FALSE. In fact, 770,000 children in the UK can't afford a healthy diet.
'*Despite our wealth, our country currently has one of the worst rates of child poverty in the European Union – ranked 21 out of 27.*'
TRUE.
'*About 85% of mums and dads who are poor find that paying for school uniform is the most expensive thing related to bringing up a child.*'
FALSE. In fact, 85% of parents living in poverty find that paying bills is the most expensive thing related to bringing up a child.
'*About 650,000 UK kids live in homes that aren't heated properly.*'
TRUE.

⇨ The above information is reprinted with kind permission from Save the Children. Visit www.savethechildren.org.uk for more information.

© *Save the Children*

Disadvantage and achievement

Disadvantaged children up to a year behind by the age of three

Many children from disadvantaged backgrounds are already up to a year behind more privileged youngsters educationally by the age of three, a UK-wide study has found.

Vocabulary scores achieved by more than 12,000 children revealed that the sons and daughters of graduates were 101 months ahead of those with the least-educated parents

Vocabulary scores achieved by more than 12,000 children revealed that the sons and daughters of graduates were 12 months ahead of those with the least-educated parents. A second 'school readiness' assessment measuring understanding of colours, letters, numbers, sizes and shapes that was given to more than 11,500 three-year-olds found an even wider gap – 13 months – between the two groups. The equivalent gaps for children in families living above and below the poverty line used by the researchers were eight months for vocabulary and nine months for school readiness.

As expected, girls did better than boys on average. They were three months ahead on both measures. Less predictably, Scots children were two months ahead of the UK average in their language development and two months ahead in 'school readiness'.

The assessments were conducted on behalf of the Centre for Longitudinal Studies, which is based at the Institute of Education, University of London. They form part of the Millennium Cohort Study (MCS), which is tracking more than 15,500 children born in 2000-2.

The assessments also highlighted marked ethnic differences. A quarter of the Black Caribbean and Black African children who took the school readiness assessment were delayed in their development, compared with only four per cent of White children.

Bangladeshi and Pakistani three-year-olds recorded relatively low scores on both tests. Their vocabulary scores were, on average, well below those normally expected for two-and-a-half-year-olds, even though non-English speakers were not included in the assessments. Bangladeshi children's school readiness scores were about a year behind those of White youngsters and Pakistani children did only slightly better.

Dr Kirstine Hansen, research director of the MCS, emphasised, however, that the assessments might not be a fair indicator of minority ethnic children's current or future ability. 'Before drawing firm conclusions we will need to investigate the circumstances in which the assessments were done, allowing for whether children lived in homes where English was not the main language spoken. There may also be cultural differences in children's readiness to attempt such tasks or engage with an unfamiliar visitor. However, it is fair to comment that teachers need to be aware that many – but by no means all – Bangladeshi and Pakistani children may do poorly on similar assessments.'
11 June 2007

⇨ The above information is reprinted with kind permission from the Centre for Longitudinal Studies, Institute of Education. Visit www.cls.ioe.ac.uk for more information.
© *Institute of Education, University of London*

Mind the gap

Divisions between rich and poor children persist but education can break the cycle of poverty, says Martin Narey

We like to assume that our children's lives will be better than ours, that they will have opportunities which we could only dream of when we were young.

This assumption may hold for our own children, but for those who are unlucky enough to be born into poverty, the reverse is true. There is increasing evidence that social mobility in the UK has stalled. And what happens at school is absolutely central to this.

Education is arguably the most powerful tool we have for breaking the cycle of poverty – stopping the misery of poverty, which taints the lives of 3.8 million children in the UK – passing from one generation to the next.

Educational disadvantage starts at a very young age – recent research indicates that children from impoverished backgrounds fall behind children born to parents who are financially more comfortable at 22 months. By the age of three, children from disadvantaged backgrounds are already up to a year behind their more advantaged peers. This gap widens as they progress through school. By the time they reach 14, many disadvantaged children are two years behind their classmates, and are destined for a lifetime of under-achievement.

This matters because how well a child does in school has long-term implications for the individual and for society. Young people who leave school with few if any qualifications are more likely to be unemployed or end up in a low skilled, low paid job, more likely to get pregnant younger, more likely to get involved in drug and alcohol abuse and more serious crime.

More than 10 per cent of 16- to 18-year-olds are not in education, employment or training (or 'Neet'), a disproportionate number of them from disadvantaged backgrounds. The government is hoping to address the Neet problem through a new bill, announced in the Queen's speech, which will require young people to stay on in education or training until they are 18. Barnardo's welcomes that bill and the intentions behind it.

> By the time they reach 14, many disadvantaged children are two years behind their classmates, and are destined for a lifetime of under-achievement

But much more is needed from this government and on two fronts – tackling child poverty as an urgent priority and at the same time, ensuring that we have an education system which helps disadvantaged children catch up rather than, as at present, seeing them fall further and further behind.

First, poverty.

The Labour government's commitment to halve child poverty by 2010 and then to eradicate it within a generation was one of the most important and inspiring pledges made in the optimistic days following the 1997 election.

Early progress was made – since 1999 more than half a million children have been lifted out of poverty. Worryingly that progress now appears to be stalling and numbers in child poverty began to rise again last year. By the government's own measures, poverty is a daily reality for one in three children in the UK, including more than half of all children in inner London often only streets away from the wealth generated by the City.

Poverty undermines children's chances in school and beyond in so many ways.

Parental qualifications and employment status influence how well children do in school. London has by far the highest proportion of children living in households where neither parent is in work. One-third of children in inner London now live in workless households.

Poor families do not have the luxury of being able to pay for extra tuition to help their children catch up or to boost their results in critical tests or exams. They cannot afford the regular evening and weekend activities such as sport, art, music or dance that their classmates enjoy. Such opportunities have a positive influence on both behaviour and academic results.

More insidiously, poverty puts great pressure on families, contributing to higher levels of conflict, family breakdown, substance abuse and domestic violence. Naturally this affects children's ability to cope in class, as well as their own emotional well-being.

Poor living conditions – crowded and damp housing, an unhealthy diet, no quiet space to do homework, no safe place to play – also add to their struggle.

For these reasons, tackling child poverty is absolutely key to narrowing the achievement gap. But we also need to do more, much more, to ensure that our education system delivers for disadvantaged children.

What more is needed to break the link between poverty and educational under-achievement? The good news is that many of the building blocks are already in place. SureStart children's centres, the new emphasis on 'personalised learning' backed by resources for extra tuition where pupils are falling behind and other reforms are all steps in the right direction.

But there are sterner challenges to be faced and a significant one is approaching fast. Some of the most disadvantaged children and young people are those who have been in care. Their only crime is to have been born to parents who either cannot or will not look after them properly. We step in as so-called Corporate Parents and do a rotten job with only 11% of children in care getting five GCSEs and only a small minority making it to university. One reason is that, almost invariably, children in care go to the worst schools, the schools most of us ensure our children don't have to go to.

The children and young persons bill, announced by the Queen, gives the government the chance to stop this and deliver on their promise that children in care will go to the best, not the worst schools. The result, at very little financial cost, will be that many more children in care will succeed at school. The challenge after that will be to provide an education system that can achieve the same for all disadvantaged children.

⇨ *Martin Narey is the chief executive of Barnardo's and chairs the Campaign to End Child Poverty.*
9 November 2007

One in five UK families can't afford heating

Nearly one in five UK households with children have had to endure cold because they can't afford the bills, a new YouGov poll for Save the Children UK has revealed

The YouGov poll revealed 19% of adults with children aged 17 or under have suffered from cold homes because of the cost of energy. 15% of households have cut back on food, and the same proportion has had to cut back on essential clothing in order to pay fuel bills.

The problem is severe among the least well-off – 44% of families living on incomes of less than £15,000 per year reported suffering from cold because of high energy prices.

One reason the UK's poorest families are hit hardest is because many rely on prepayment meters to heat their homes – which cost significantly more than paying fuel bills by Direct Debit.

'Fuel poverty is an outrage, particularly for children,' said Phillipa Hunt, UK Poverty Spokesperson at Save the Children. 'It means that they are experiencing the effects of cold on a daily basis. Children find it more difficult to do their homework in a cold home, and are more likely to suffer ill health.

'The government is well behind schedule in its promise of halving child poverty by 2010 and ending it by 2020,' she said. 'To achieve the 2010 target the government needs to invest £4 billion to help the poorest families. As part of the Campaign to End Child Poverty, we are calling on the government to use this Budget to invest a significant proportion of this money.

'Save the Children is also campaigning for seasonal grants, in winter and in the summer, of £100 per child for the poorest families,' she continued. 'This would help relieve the increased costs at these expensive times of year.'

Pre-pay vs. Direct Debit

Research also reveals a major reason why so many households with the lowest incomes are unable to heat their homes properly – the poorest pay more for energy.

In comparison with the cost of paying for electricity and gas with a pre-payment meter, and paying for it by online Direct Debit, it was found that on average pre-pay meters are 26% more expensive: an extra £215 every year.

The worst offender is British Gas. For electricity it charges 58% more for pre-pay compared with online Direct Debit – £159 more on average per year. For gas, pre-pay customers are charged 47% more compared with their online Direct Debit customers – £228 more every year for the average customer.

'We know that less well-off families

are much more likely to use pre-pay meters, because it gives them the flexibility to plan a weekly budget,' said Phillipa Hunt. 'So by charging more for using pre-pay meters, energy companies are in fact penalising those families and children who are least able to pay.'

'We want energy companies to bring their pre-pay charges in line with the cost of online Direct Debit.

'The government also needs to play its part. It should use the new Energy Bill to enforce minimum standards of social tariffs, so that people on low incomes are paying as little as possible

for their energy,' Ms Hunt added.
5 February 2008

⇨ The above information is reprinted with kind permission from Save the Children. Visit www. savethechildren.org.uk for more.
© Save the Children

What are benefits?

Information from askcab

What are benefits?
We use the term 'benefits' to describe any money that is given to us by the government. Benefits are paid to any member of the public, who may need extra money to help them meet the costs of everyday living.

What benefits are there?
Although there are many different types of benefit available, they can all be broken down into two main types. These are:
⇨ Means-tested benefits, and
⇨ Non-means-tested benefits.

Means-tested benefits will take into account your income (how much you get paid) and any savings that you may have. Means-tested benefits are then paid out, providing that your income and savings are sufficiently low enough.

Non-means-tested benefits do not rely on your income or savings, but your individual circumstances will affect whether your claim will be successful.

There are two main types of non-means-tested benefits. These are known as:
⇨ Contributory benefits, and
⇨ Non-contributory benefits.

You will become eligible for contributory benefits providing that you have made sufficient National Insurance contributions over a specific period of time.

Non-contributory benefits are paid for through the tax system, and as a result, will not rely on your contribution record.

So what are they for?
There are many different kinds of benefit available. Each one has been

designed to pay out under specific circumstances. There are benefits available to cover:
⇨ Unemployment;
⇨ Sickness;
⇨ Disability;
⇨ Housing Issues;
⇨ Pregnancy;
⇨ Education;
⇨ Raising a family;
⇨ and many more.

We use the term 'benefits' to describe any money that is given to us by the government

---

It may even be that you are already eligible for some form of financial help because of your circumstances. If any of the above circumstances apply to your current situation, then you should enquire about claiming a benefit.

For more information and activities on benefits please visit www. doughuk.com

Who deals with benefit claims?
There are several government bodies throughout the country that deal with the distribution of certain benefits. These include the Inland Revenue, the Jobcentre plus agency, and local authorities (local councils).

The agency that you will need to contact will depend on the benefit that you are making a claim for. The A to Z of benefits section of the site will tell you which agencies deal with a particular benefit, and will also

provide you with information on how to apply.

It is important that you realise that the benefits system is a very complicated one, and if you find that you have trouble understanding your entitlement, or if you feel that you need help at any stage of your claim, then you should seek some advice.

⇨ The above information is reprinted with kind permission from askcab. Visit www.askcab.co.uk for more information.
© askcab

BENEFITS ENQUIRIES

Benefit claims and poverty

£14 billion of means-tested benefits fails to reach those in poverty

New figures released today by DWP estimate that up to £9.4 billion is not being claimed in means-tested benefits by those who are entitled to it. This shows a further decrease in take-up on last year's figures.

Earlier this year HM Revenue and Customs figures revealed that up to £4.5 billion of Working Tax Credit and Child Tax Credit goes unclaimed annually, making a total of up to around £14 billion a year that those in greatest need of support are not receiving.

CPAG's Chief Executive Kate Green said:

'With child poverty having increased recently for the first time in years, it is of great concern that take-up of means tested benefits is continuing to fall.

'It is particularly concerning that take-up of income-based Jobseeker's Allowance has fallen by 13% over recent years, as this is a gateway for the poorest families to other benefits. Not enough is being done to understand and address this urgent problem.

'Reliance on means testing has become too great and is failing. The complexity of benefits and tax credits is proving to be too great a barrier for millions who should be receiving support. If the Government continues to rely primarily on means-tested support to reach its targets for ending child poverty, it will fail. Ministers must look again at the role of universal benefits like Child Benefit.

'The Government must accept the Work and Pensions Committee's call for a Welfare Commission to undertake a fundamental review aimed at producing a simpler, fairer system that does not leave so many poor families missing out on essential support.'

Notes

⇨ The ONS announcement on Income Related Benefits Estimates of Take-Up in 2005-06 can be found here: http://www.dwp.gov.uk/mediacentre/pressreleases/2007/sep/ifd130907benefits.pdf

⇨ The HM Revenue and Customs report on take-up of Working Tax Credit can be found here: http://www.hmrc.gov.uk/stats/personal-tax-credits/takeup-rates2004-05.pdf

13 September 2007

⇨ Information from the Child Poverty Action Group. Visit www.cpag.org.uk for more.

© Child Poverty Action Group

Welfare shake-up scraps incapacity benefit

Reforms of the welfare system including a replacement of the incapacity benefit and 'more responsibility' for claimants have been announced by the government.

The welfare green paper had been played up as a revolutionary series of changes before its official announcement by senior ministers.

And, announcing the green paper to the Commons this afternoon, work and pensions secretary James Purnell claimed it was completing the government's welfare reforms begun ten years ago.

An effectively temporary employment support allowance will replace incapacity benefit from 2013, while full-time work is flagged up as a sanction to be used by all advisers where necessary.

After three and six months claimants will have to intensify their job searches.

Those who are jobless for over a year will be expected to undertake four weeks of community work, while the two per cent the government expects to remain unemployed after two years will be expected to enter into full-time work.

This could include community work like litter-picking.

Mr Purnell said the government sought to provide 'more support' in return for 'more responsibility'.

'We know our support works but we also know conditionality works. We can increase employment and reduce poverty,' he said.

'In the past, people were... encouraged to spend a lifetime on benefits. Once they'd signed on, the welfare system often switched off.

'This green paper ends all that. It puts us on the road to our ambition of an 80 per cent employment rate... It will transform the lives of hundreds of thousands of people.'

Among the other measures outlined are enhanced support for those suffering from drug addictions, help to ensure disabled people are put 'in control' and 'strengthened parental responsibility'.

The latter will see parents on benefits allowed to keep all their maintenance payments for the first time.

Shadow work and pensions secretary Chris Grayling said many of the proposals were 'a straight lift from our green paper published in January' but said he would support the policies.

'We look forward to trying to work with the government to turn these proposals into reality as quickly as possible,' he said.

Mr Purnell responded by pointing out the Freud report, on which much of today's proposals were based, had been commissioned by the government.

'He can scrabble around trying to get the credit if he wants to. We'll get on doing the right thing and governing the country,' Mr Purnell added.

21 July 2008

© politics.co.uk

Poverty: a 10-minute guide

Information from World Vision

What is poverty?

'Injustice anywhere is a threat to justice everywhere.' Martin Luther King

The simplest definition of poverty is a lack of the resources needed to live a 'normal life', which is linked to the unequal distribution of global wealth. But at its most fundamental, poverty is about far more than money or exchange of goods. Poverty is about the connection between people everywhere, and the effects of how these people think, act and react. Poverty is about hopes, dreams and how many people are prevented from dreaming. Poverty is made worse by the complexity of our world and its structures.

Who does poverty affect?

Like everybody else, you have probably been affected by some measure of poverty. Maybe you have noticed the cold and hungry figures huddling in a doorway in the street, or crouching on a bench in the park? Or perhaps you yourself have experience of struggling to pay the telephone bill or the rent?

In general, though, extreme poverty usually occurs in developing countries, mostly in Sub-Saharan Africa, Asia and South America. Within developing countries, some groups are even more susceptible to extreme poverty:

Women and children

The number of women living in poverty is higher than that of men and appears to be growing. In developing countries, women are usually less educated and have lower paid jobs than men. Children are always the most vulnerable section of any society. With less ability to protect and provide for themselves, they risk exploitation, abuse, hunger and disease.

Disabled people

Disability can be both a cause and effect of poverty. Disabled people often find it difficult to get work and take part in activities that most non-disabled people take for granted. This is because society tends to exclude disabled people. Disabled people are often viewed as helpless victims in need of charity, instead of citizens with equal rights. In some communities, disability is viewed as the result of a curse. Often it is the attitudes of others towards disabled people that are the major problems, rather than an individual's specific impairment. Disabled people face many barriers because of unfair policies and practices.

Indigenous peoples

According to the United Nations, indigenous peoples comprise five per cent of the global population but 12 per cent of the world's poor.

The extreme poverty experienced by these and many other people goes far beyond concerns with food, water and shelter. It impinges on personal freedoms, identity, self-respect, well-being and on the opportunity to live healthy and fulfilling lives.

'We are the first generation that can look extreme... poverty in the eye and say this and mean it – we have the cash, we have the drugs, we have the science. Do we have the will to make poverty history?' (Bono, 2004)

What causes poverty?

Poverty is largely human-made, often caused by complex issues of

---

Poverty facts

⇨ Of the world's 6.1 billion people, some 1.1 billion live in extreme poverty.

⇨ Over one billion people don't have access to clean water and are vulnerable to potentially fatal diseases.

⇨ More than two billion people do not have adequate sanitation – two million under-fives die every year from diarrhoea.

⇨ Inadequate shelter exposes poor people to the weather, pollutants and diseases transmitted by animals.

war and conflict, unfair trade laws, unjust governments, corruption and plain old-fashioned greed. Poverty is a problem because humankind allows injustice to exist. Humans have created a world where there are huge differences in quality of life, and where war and conflict are widespread. We often fail to care for our environment or speak up for the voiceless and oppressed.

But poverty is not inevitable... Children don't have to die of hunger, abuse or exploitation. A more equal world is possible. And ultimately – like poverty – equality too comes down to people's actions and choices. Making changes is all about how we choose to act. Just as importantly, it is about what we refuse to ignore.

Child focus

Naitil lives in Haiti but doesn't know how old he is. When his grandfather died, Naitil was left with no family or money and was forced to live on the streets until a lady called Hosanna took him into her own home. But unless something changes, Naitil's future seems uncertain. Unless fairer trade rules and more and improved aid allow the Haitian Government to educate and care better for its inhabitants, children like Naitil will have little chance of escaping poverty.

Jargon buster

Poverty
The term **moderate poverty** is applied to people who can meet their basic needs (food, water, housing), but who lack the resources to improve their lives. The term **extreme poverty** refers to an inability to meet even these basic survival needs.

Global inequality
The gap between the world's rich and poor is wider than ever: The richest fifth of the world's people:
⇨ consume 45 per cent of the world's meat and fish;
⇨ consume 58 per cent of the world's energy;
⇨ consume 84 per cent of all paper;
⇨ own 87 per cent of the world's vehicles.

Millennium Development Goals (MDGs)
These are a set of eight targets agreed by world leaders at the United Nations Millennium Summit in New York in 2000. They aim to make the world a better place by setting measurable objectives for poverty, health, education and the environment.

Choose change

Make personal choices
Live ethically and shop wisely. Inform yourself and your friends about poverty and how to beat it.

Support trade justice movements
Write to your MP – be unusual when you write and ask if there is any way you can help. Or become a World Vision campaigner at www.worldvision.org.uk

Learn more

⇨ Go to World Vision's website and sign up for Worldview, the monthly email newsletter. It contains lots of world-changing ideas.
⇨ Subscribe to World Vision's free magazines by calling 01908 841010.
↳ *Insight* takes a regular look at poverty-related issues around the world.
↳ *Bug* is a great way for young people to stay informed and make a difference.

Want to find out more?

CAFOD (*The Catholic Agency for Overseas Development*)
www.cafod.org.uk
A useful set of factsheets on the issues.
The Department for International Development
http://www.dfid.gov.uk
The website of the Government department responsible for the implementation of the MDGs.
The Pocket Guide to Poverty
A World Vision youth guide, available free by phoning 01908 841010.

⇨ The above information is reprinted with kind permission from World Vision. Visit www.worldvision.org.uk for more information.
© *World Vision*

Proportion of the world population in poverty

Proportion of population living on less than $1 a day (2004)

- 2-5%
- 6-20%
- 21-32%
- 33-71%
- Missing data

Source: UN 'Millennium Development Goals Indicators Database' (2007).

Life on $1 a day

What does it really mean to live on a dollar a day? Abiy Hailu, head of Christian Aid's Ethiopia programme, faces up to the reality behind the statistics

You do not need to go far to find the poor in Ethiopia – they are all around.

Begging for their survival on the streets and at traffic lights in the capital, Addis Ababa: the sick, the elderly, the disabled, mothers with children. Sleeping rough out in the open, through heavy rain and cold.

The poor of the Addis streets test your conscience. Whether to give alms and, if so, to whom, is a decision you make every day. But it is never a comfortable one.

What strikes me about these people is their anonymity. I wonder sometimes whether they are even part of the United Nations poverty statistics – the ones that tell us officially how many people are trying to get by on less than a dollar a day.

I do not know how they cope with life. How do they get treatment when they are ill? Do they even have someone to bury them when they die?

Yet they are people like you and me. And they are everywhere. I have been tempted to find out more about them. What aspirations do they have? How did they get into the condition they are in? Do they want to break out and take their destiny into their own hands?

The anonymous poor

These are the 'anonymous poor'. But the story of poverty does not end here. There are also those with a roof over their heads who are otherwise almost equally badly off. They may try to keep their dignity and refrain from begging, but the odds are against them.

Some are my own close family members. They live in poor accommodation, in poor neighbourhoods. Just getting to their homes along unlit, muddy tracks in the rainy season and in the evenings is a hazardous undertaking.

Ato Fanta, 75, is a retired security guard from one such neighbourhood. He and his wife have two daughters and many grandchildren. They also have custody of children from their sons who have died. Whenever I visit the Fanta family, there are no fewer than seven or eight mouths to feed.

Ato Fanta has only a small pension, about 200 birr (£12.50) per month, and the contribution from the two working children (who have their own families) is negligible.

Globally, people are said to be in poverty if they have less than $1 a day to live on

How do they cope with so little income? How do they afford school books and uniforms, or get treatment when they fall ill? And how, despite their deprivation, do they not only appreciate visits, but also receive me with generosity?

Average income: 15 pence a day

For the Fanta family, an income of a dollar a day would actually mean a step up in the world. For seven of them, that would be $7 a day, or about £4 – a very respectable income.

I doubt whether the Fanta family attain even a third of this in a country where the average income is only $100 a year – barely 15 pence a day.

Given that so many families are living in such poverty you may wonder whether aid is working at all. But Christian Aid's partners are making a significant difference in the communities in which they work.

In the countryside they are helping strengthen people's livelihoods and providing safe drinking water. Household hygiene and therefore health are improving dramatically because of a reduction in water-borne diseases.

They are also helping farmers to manage their environment better through water and soil conservation. More fertile soil is producing better crops and thus increased income.

But what those anonymous faces on the streets of Addis tell me is that we have such a long way to go. Because, for the thousands of families we are lifting out of poverty, there are thousands more that we have yet to reach.

More than money

What is needed is not just money, although that would help.

I believe we also need to awaken much more interest among the general public in the plight of the poor in countries such as Ethiopia.

The more interest there is, the more people can appreciate that we are all citizens of one world, with the sense of solidarity and equal rights and responsibilities that entails. Only then might we see the levels of giving, praying and campaigning for change which Ethiopia's poorest people so need.

⇨ *Christian Aid gave nearly £325,000 to support agricultural and clean water projects in Ethiopia in 2005/06.*

⇨ The above information is re-printed with kind permission from Christian Aid. Visit www.christianaid.org.uk for more information.

Christian Aid © 2006

Global poverty

Information from World Vision UK

A world of inequality

Every day, the gap between rich and poor seems to get just that little bit wider. For millions of people poverty does not just mean a lack of money, but malnutrition, hunger, disease and a lack of education. Poverty causes the young, the old and the vulnerable to die early. And the cycle of poverty can seem inescapable.

Poverty is about a shortage of resources and an inability to meet basic needs. But it is also about people, the connections between them, and how they think, act and react. Poverty is a problem because we live in a world of inequality where many people are denied the opportunity to live safe and fulfilling lives.

But things can get better! The solution, like the problem, is in our hands. We can right wrongs. Injustices can be overcome. Lives can change forever and we only have to take it one step at a time.

How poor is poor?

Globally, people are described as living in poverty if they have less than US$1 a day to live on. Imagine if that was all the money you had each day – it's barely enough to buy a loaf of bread or carton of milk, let alone pay the rent or buy clothes.

Although we use income as a measure of poverty, many of the poorest people never even have money in their hands. Often they survive on what they can manage to grow on a small plot of land. They may try to barter, or beg, or even scavenge on rubbish dumps just to survive.

Food and water

Hunger is one of the most obvious signs of poverty – when people can't get basic nutrients for a healthy, active life. Chronic hunger and malnutrition stunt growth and make people vulnerable to disease. In countries where hunger is most common, one in seven children will die before the age of five.

Having clean water is another measure of how poor a person is. More than one billion people in the world don't have access to safe water. More than two million people in developing countries – most of them children – die every year from diseases related to dirty water, inadequate sanitation and poor hygiene.

Literacy and life expectancy

Literacy, the ability to read and write, is another way poverty is measured. It's important because if people are not literate, they are left out of many forms of communication. And they struggle to get well-paid jobs. Most people who are illiterate live in poor countries. In 2000, one in five adults aged over 15 was illiterate. Women accounted for two out of three of these.

For millions of people poverty does not just mean a lack of money, but malnutrition, hunger, disease and a lack of education

---

Lack of good nutrition, clean water and education ultimately shorten a person's life. In rich countries like the UK, the average person can expect to live to the age of 78. In poor countries, a person can expect to live 20 years less – an average of 59 years. In very poor regions, like sub-Saharan Africa, life expectancy is as low as 35 years.

One change leads to many

If none of the factors that create poverty are changed, people can't do anything about the situation that keeps them poor. But changing just one of those factors can have a dramatic effect. For example, if clean water is available close to home, girls no longer need to spend hours collecting it. They will have time to go to school instead. And they'll be healthy enough because they are less likely to be sick from diseases like diarrhoea.

Research shows that babies of educated women tend to be healthier and, in turn, better educated. Women who earn a living are more likely to put money back into health and education for their families. Ultimately, whole communities benefit when girls have the opportunity for education. All this change – just from having clean water!

The Millennium Development Goals

In 2000, world leaders decided that they needed a strategy to tackle poverty. They set and agreed targets, which are called the Millennium Development Goals. These targets aim to halve poverty and hunger, promote equal opportunity and improve health.

The goals are:
⇨ wipe out extreme poverty and hunger.
⇨ make primary education available to all children.
⇨ get more girls into secondary education and empower women.
⇨ reduce the number of children who die before their fifth birthday.
⇨ reduce the number of women dying in childbirth.
⇨ combat HIV and AIDS, malaria and other diseases.
⇨ care for the environment – including more access to safe water, and better homes for slum dwellers.
⇨ work together to tackle poverty.

If these goals were met, our world would be a very different place. The goals are tangible and achievable. But both rich countries and developing countries need to do more to meet them.

⇨ The above information is reprinted with kind permission from World Vision UK. Visit www.worldvision.org.uk for more information.

© World Vision UK

Facts and figures

In a world where a few hundred millionaires own as much wealth as the world's poorest 2.5 billion people, poverty is a choice made by the rich, not by the poor

Get angry
⇨ More than 8 million people die each year from abject poverty.
⇨ Half the world – nearly three billion people – live on less than $2 a day.
⇨ Almost a billion people entered the 21st century unable to read or sign their names.
⇨ 852 million people do not have enough to eat, 1.3 billion have no safe water, 2 billion have no access to electricity and 3 billion have no sanitation.

More than 8 million people die each year from abject poverty

⇨ Hunger and malnutrition are the number one risk to global health, killing more people than AIDS, malaria and TB put together.

Children are the future – aren't they?
⇨ Of the 2.2 billion children in the world, one billion – almost half – live in poverty.
⇨ 10.9 million children die every year before they reach the age of five.
⇨ A child dies every five seconds because she or he is hungry.
⇨ Every year, 17 million children are born undernourished because their mothers don't have enough to eat.
⇨ More than a billion children will not go to school this year – 65% of them girls.

Who ate all the pies?
⇨ 51 of the world's 100 wealthiest bodies are corporations.
⇨ A few hundred millionaires own as much wealth as the world's poorest 2.5 billion people.

⇨ The combined economic output of a quarter of the world's countries is less than the wealth of the world's three richest men.

Who lives? Who dies?
⇨ In Bolivia and Peru, babies are four to five times as likely to die if they are born in the poorest 20% of the population than the richest 20%.
⇨ 80% of all Ethiopians live on less than two dollars a day – and 26% on less than a dollar.
⇨ Life expectancy in Afghanistan is just 43 years.

It's a matter of choice
⇨ Just one week's worth of the subsidies given to farmers in rich countries would cover the annual cost of global food aid.
⇨ $20 billion is spent on cosmetics in the United States each year – more than double the $9 billion it would take to provide basic water and sanitation for everyone.
⇨ Annual global military spending exceeds $1 trillion. That's a thousand billion dollars – around 100 times what it would cost to put every child in the world through primary school.

⇨ The above information is re-printed with kind permission from Christian Aid. Visit www.christianaid.org.uk for more information.
Christian Aid © 2006

Public attitudes to international aid

Respondents were asked: 'The actual percentage of UK government spend on aid in 2005-2006 was 1.3 per cent of all government spend, which equates to £4.4 billion. Knowing this, do you think the UK Government spends too much, too little or about the right amount on international aid?'

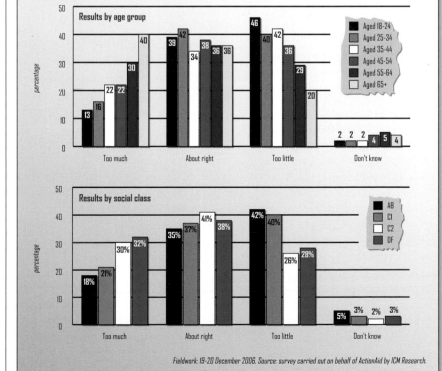

Fieldwork: 19-20 December 2006. Source: survey carried out on behalf of ActionAid by ICM Research.

Poverty, hunger and disease

So much done yet so much left to do

The millennium development goals set by the UN at the turn of the century made up the most aspirational development programme ever devised. But a progress report published today by Unicef says that even though more babies are surviving, more children are in school and fewer families live in poverty, urgent action is needed if the goals are to be met by the target date of 2015. Here Sarah Boseley and Larry Elliott look at seven of the goals and assess how much progress has been made.

Goal 1: To eradicate extreme poverty and hunger

Targets by 2015 To halve the proportion of people in 1990 who were suffering from hunger. To halve the proportion of people whose income is less than $1 a day

---

143 million children under five in the developing world continue to suffer from inadequate nutrition

---

To monitor the fight against hunger, the UN took as its yardstick the proportion of children under five who are underweight. In 1990, 32% of under-fives in the developing world were underweight, undernourished and therefore at high risk of stunted growth, disease and death. Today that figure has come down, but not by much, to 27%. East Asia, the Pacific and eastern Europe have made the biggest advances and 58 countries are on target to reach the millennium development goal.

But 143 million children under five in the developing world continue to suffer from inadequate nutrition. The highest numbers are in south Asia, where over half the under-fives (54%) were underweight in 1990, but there is progress in this region, with the proportion falling to 46% by 2006. Asia, the second poorest part of the globe, has seen a drop from 41.1% living below the poverty line to 29.5% by 2004. However, there have been no such gains in sub-Saharan Africa. If progress continues to be this slow and patchy, the 2015 target will be missed by a margin of 30 million children.

Poverty is more widespread in sub-Saharan Africa than anywhere else: in 1990, 46.8% of people were on less than $1 a day. That had reduced to 41.1% by 2004. Because of Asia's rapid economic growth, the overall level of poverty has been cut from 31.6% in the developing world to 19.2% and if this continues, the global target will be met, although Asia's success is masking the lack of progress in sub-Saharan Africa.

Progress report Target on poverty likely to be reached, but goal on hunger is unlikely.

Goal 2: To achieve universal primary education

Target To ensure that, by 2015, children everywhere, both boys and girls, will be able to complete a full course of primary schooling

The two indicators used to monitor progress in meeting this goal are the percentage of children enrolled in primary school and those who complete this stage of education by reaching grade five or 'primary completion rate'. Both developed and developing countries have put considerable effort into achieving the education goal and the Unicef report says there has been 'substantial progress'. Partly as a result of debt cancellation, countries such as Tanzania are on course to achieve 100% primary participation by 2015, although sub-Saharan Africa as a whole will not meet the target without more rapid progress over the next seven years. The UK has a 10-year £10bn programme for education in developing countries.

According to the Unicef report, more than 85% of primary school-age children are now receiving a basic education, although the figure drops to 70% in eastern and southern Africa and just 62% in west and central Africa. Between 2002 and 2005, the number of children out of school dropped from 115 million to 93 million, and of those still without a school place 41 million live in sub-Saharan Africa and a further 31.5 million live in south Asia.

Actual attendance rates tend to be lower than enrolment rates. In eastern Africa, for example, fewer than three out of five children attend primary school, and Unicef says that some of those are pupils of secondary school age who have started their education late or are retaking grades. For countries nearing universal primary education, Unicef says that reaching the last 10% of children out of school is a 'particular challenge'.

Progress report There are 86 countries in the world that have yet to achieve universal primary education. On current trends 58 will still not have done so by 2015. Even so, there are hopes that progress will be speeded up, with attention in the better performing countries now switching to quality of education and expansion of secondary schooling.

Goal 3: To promote gender equality and empower women

Target To eliminate gender disparity in primary and secondary education, preferably by 2005, and in all levels of education no later than 2015

The gap between boys and girls receiving a primary education narrowed between 1990 and 2005 – from 8 percentage points to 4 percentage points – but Unicef says big gender disparities remain, particularly in west and central Africa, the Middle East and north Africa, and south Asia. Only two-thirds of countries met the target of gender parity in primary education by 2005, with one-third achieving gender parity in secondary education. Gender disparities are greatest in rural areas and among poor households.

Progress report The gender equality target is unlikely to be met on current trends, even though Unicef says it is just a starting point towards the eventual goal of education being a 'fulfilling experience for all girls and boys'.

Goal 4: To reduce child mortality

Target To reduce by two-thirds, between 1990 and 2015, the under-five mortality rate

Unicef recently celebrated the passing of a milestone in the battle to reduce the death toll among babies in the developing world. In 2006, for the first time since records were kept, the number of children dying before their fifth birthday dropped below 10 million a year, to 9.7 million.

Poverty is more widespread in sub-Saharan Africa than anywhere else: in 1990, 46.8% of people were on less than $1 a day

---

But baby deaths are still distressingly commonplace. The death rate is substantially higher in sub-Saharan Africa than elsewhere. In 1990, 187 babies and children under five died there for every 1,000 births. By last year, that had been reduced, but only to 160 per 1,000 births. South Asia has the next highest death rate, but has been making significant progress, dropping from 123 per 1,000 births in 1990 to 83.

The stakes are high. If the millennium development goal target is reached by 2015, 5.4 million children's lives will be saved in that year alone. Most deaths occur during and shortly after birth (37%), but preventable diseases also take a big toll. Pneumonia kills 19%, diarrhoea 17% and malaria 8%.

One bright spot has been the success of routine measles vaccination, which cut measles deaths by 75% in sub-Saharan Africa between 1999 and 2005. And when mothers bring their babies to be vaccinated, they are being offered other life-saving interventions at the clinic, such as bed nets to protect against malaria, deworming medicines and vitamin A.

Progress report A long way off target.

Goal 5: To improve maternal health

Target To reduce by three-quarters the 1990 maternal mortality ratio

Every year, half a million women die in pregnancy or childbirth, almost all of them in sub-Saharan Africa and Asia. Having a baby is a very high risk in southern Africa. According to the latest figures published today by Unicef, a woman has a one in 22 lifetime chance of dying in pregnancy or childbirth, compared with one in 8,000 in countries like the UK.

It has proved very difficult to get accurate figures for maternal deaths in the developing world. Many countries have no system of death registration, and death from diseases such as Aids or malaria will not be added to the maternal mortality count, even though they are made more likely by pregnancy.

Experts believe that the global rate of maternal mortality did come down between 1990 and 2005, but only by about 5.4%. To reach the target, the death rate would have to come down by about that much every year.

But not even this small rate of progress is being achieved in sub-Saharan Africa, according to a report from the World Bank, the World Health Organisation, Unicef and the UN Population Fund, which claims that the numbers of maternal deaths actually rose in sub-Saharan Africa from 212,000 a year to 270,000 over that period (although there was negligible change in the maternal mortality rate because live births also increased).

More than a third of the deaths are caused by haemorrhage and 16% by blood poisoning and infections including Aids. Skilled birth attendants are key to reducing deaths, but sub-Saharan Africa has only managed to increase their presence at births from 43% to 47% and South Asia from 31% to 40%.

However, antenatal care has

improved in all regions. Preventing unplanned pregnancies could cut deaths by a quarter, but only 23% of sub-Saharan African women use any form of contraception.

Progress report A long way off target.

Goal 6: To combat HIV and Aids, malaria and other diseases

Target To halt and begin to reverse the spread of HIV and Aids. To halt and begin to reverse the incidence of malaria and other major diseases

The percentage of people living with HIV/Aids levelled off for the first time this year, UNAids said last month, at 33.2 million (less than last year's estimate because of a big revision in the figures). The number of new infections fell to 2.5 million and is now thought to have peaked in the late 1990s, when it was more than 3 million a year. But the total number of people living with HIV continues to rise, as people survive longer thanks to treatment. Efforts to educate young people about protecting themselves from HIV and encourage condom use have not been very successful. Only 24% of 15- to 24-year-olds in low and middle income countries have a comprehensive understanding of HIV.

Malaria kills more than a million people a year, 80% of them children under five in sub-Saharan Africa. Africa has widely adopted, in principle, new antimalarial drugs recommended by the WHO, but they are not always given to the children who need them. While 16 out of 20 countries have tripled their use of bed nets to protect against bites from carrier mosquitoes, only a handful came close to the target of 60% bed net coverage set in 2000, and in sub-Saharan Africa only 5% of small children sleep under them.

Progress report Could reach target, but too soon to say.

Goal 7: To ensure environmental sustainability

Target To halve, between 1990 and 2015, the proportion without sustainable access to basic sanitation

With health and education given priority, sanitation has been the forgotten millennium development goal. Although sanitation coverage increased from 49% in 1990 to 59% in 2004, progress has been far too slow to meet the UN's goal and the Unicef report says that on current trends the target will be missed by more than half a billion people. This is despite the fact that the UN itself says that there is a direct link between sanitation and achieving the other goals.

Lack of sanitation, poor hygiene and unsafe drinking water cause the deaths of more than 1.5 million children every year from diarrhoeal diseases and lead to millions of children, particularly girls, being kept off school.

The latest figures, for 2004, show that 2.6 billion people – almost half the world's population – lack access to proper sanitation and Unicef admits that simply keeping pace with population growth remains a huge challenge. This is especially true in sub-Saharan Africa, where the number of people without access to sanitation has increased by 100 million since 1990.

Progress report With Unicef admitting that a lack of political support is a 'major barrier to progress', the sanitation goal is one of the least likely to be hit, and will not be achieved for another 70 years on current trends.

10 December 2007

It's a question of debt

Information from the Jubilee Debt Campaign

There are many big issues that demand our attention today. Every time we turn on the television we are bombarded with adverts telling us what we need to live a so-called fulfilled life. The pressure to get more money, to buy more stuff, can be very great. But for some people, the issue isn't whether or not to buy the latest pair of trainers, but where they will find the money to buy enough food to be able to survive.

Poverty is one of the biggest issues facing our world today. And one of the big issues which influences poverty, is DEBT.

But what is debt?

In its simplest form, debt is credit. When someone offers you instant credit, they are offering you instant debt. When someone lends you 50p, you owe them 50p. You are 50p in debt to them.

In the commercial and business world, people borrow money and have to pay it back with interest. For example, if I lend you £100 at 10% interest, you will owe me £110. The higher the interest rate, the more you will owe. So remember, if someone wants to give you credit, what they're really saying is that they will sell you something, or lend you money, but they will want more back in return. So, if in the future you wanted to buy a computer, a car, or a house, you could get a mortgage, pay by credit card, get a loan from a bank, or you can get it on 'instant credit'. Whatever it is, you will have to pay back more than the cost of the stuff you're buying.

Which is fine when you can afford to repay the loan: but what happens when you can't? You simply have to pay more interest, take out another loan to repay the first one, sell things to make the money, or go without. The poorest people often have to repay debt at the highest prices, and can't afford to buy food and other essentials.

Why is it an international issue?

Just like people, countries borrow money, and some of the poorest countries borrowed money in the 1970s when interest rates were low. But interest rates have increased and the poor countries can't afford to pay back the interest on their loans, never mind the loans themselves. Because of this, they simply owe more each year and have slipped further into debt. The richer countries and institutions like the International Monetary Fund and World Bank also offered the poorer countries more loans to 'help' them pay off their debt, thus putting them further into debt.

John Simpson, BBC journalist, said: 'We have piled a mountain of debt on the poorest and most vulnerable countries in the world: countries which, on the other side of the ledger, we regard as being most in need of our assistance. It has become the modern equivalent of slavery.'

Cardinal Hume, Archbishop of Westminster, said: 'Whatever the detailed history of today's debt-ridden countries, nearly all have one key factor in common: that those who could be blamed the least, the poorest people in the poorest countries, have suffered the most.'

Life and debt

There is no doubt about it: poverty and debt are linked. Because of debt, some of the poorest countries in the world are paying rich countries far more in debt repayments than they are getting in aid. Jubilee Debt Campaign calculates that developing countries are paying around £600 million per day in debt repayments. For every pound developing countries received in grants, they pay out over £2 to repay their debts. Because countries have to pay out so much in debt repayments, they can't spend money on essential services, like healthcare, education, water and sanitation. The result is greater poverty and death. Right now, one billion people live without access to safe drinking water.

Actor Ewan McGregor said: 'Before going to Africa I knew a bit about the debt burden but I was staggered by how the massive amount of what has to be paid back affects people. It's not just capital; it's vast amounts of interest. It's just insane. There are kids starving to death and countries aren't allowed to support their people because they're too busy selling crops to earn money to pay us back – and we don't even need it!'

In 2004, Malawi paid £60 million in debt repayments after debt relief, despite its near famine. The country had been encouraged by the World Bank and International Monetary Fund to sell maize reserves to make debt repayments. But debt relief for Malawi has been delayed because the World Bank says it has spent too much. Malawi had to increase spending to buy emergency grain to prevent a famine.

U2's Bono said (during a CNN interview): '. . . a lot of the poorest countries are still paying more servicing old debts than they are on healthcare and education. That's unacceptable. Health, and particularly HIV/AIDS and malaria, set back development 20 years. There is no point in us cancelling their debts if there's no one there.'

'While eight million die each year for want of the funds spent by the rich countries on their pets; when millions of children stay out of school for want of half a percent of the US defence budget; and when the amount spent on alcohol in a week and a half in Europe would be adequate to provide sanitation to half the world's population, something is very wrong . . . more than a billion people do not need to live in poverty while their debts are being repaid.'
The Unbreakable Link. Debt Relief and the Millennium Development Goals, 2002 Jubilee Debt Campaign and New Economics Foundation

⇨ The above information is reprinted with kind permission from Jubilee Debt Campaign. Visit www.jubileedebtcampaign.org.uk for more information.

© *Jubilee Debt Campaign*

Facts

⇨ Altogether, developing countries pay around £600 million every day to the rich world.

⇨ For every £1 that poor countries receive in aid, they pay out more than £2 in debt service.

⇨ Africa gets £36 million each day in aid. In 2005, Comic Relief's Red Nose Day raised £37 million. But every day Africa pays £28 million to the rich world.

⇨ In 2004, Malawi had to pay nearly £6 per person servicing debt, even though it can spend only about £3 per person on health. Average life expectancy in Malawi is just 37 and one in seven adults is HIV positive.

⇨ Countries have to comply with harsh conditions to get debt relief – meaning that Zambia, for instance, could not afford to pay for around 9,000 new teachers that it desperately needs.

⇨ However, thanks to debt cancellation, many countries are now paying out less to the rich and spending more on health and education. For instance, debt cancellation has paid for training 3,600 new teachers every year in Malawi, 2,000 new schools in Tanzania, a free childhood immunisation programme in Mozambique, and HIV / AIDS programmes in Benin. But more is needed!

Aid questions and answers

Information from ActionAid

Who pays for international aid?

The majority of aid to developing countries comes from the governments of wealthy countries. The internationally agreed target for how much a government should give in aid is 0.7% of gross national income – although only a few countries have reached this level. Governments direct their aid in a number of different ways – from spending it through multilateral institutions like the World Bank or EU, to giving it directly to the government of a developing country, or channelling it through NGOs such as ActionAid. The way donor governments decide to spend their aid has huge implications for how effective it is at tackling poverty and promoting development. At present, too much aid is designed to primarily benefit rich countries, rather than to promote development.

Does more aid mean less poverty?

While giving aid to poor communities or countries undoubtedly improves the lives of millions of people around the world every year, simply giving more aid money is not enough to break the cycle of poverty. The aid which governments do provide at the moment must be much better quality – so that it focuses on tackling the root causes of poverty. Developing countries need to have a much bigger say in the international decisions which affect them directly. At the moment, international institutions like the WTO or IMF (which are controlled by rich countries) are able to force developing countries to adopt risky and unsuitable policies – such as rapid trade liberalisation – which hurt the poorest.

Doesn't most aid go to corrupt politicians?

While political and economic corruption is a major problem in many developing countries, it is important to remember that corruption is a symptom of poverty – not its main cause. Poor and excluded people around the world are already demanding an end to corruption, and it is vital that we support them in this struggle. Corruption isn't just down to politicians in developing countries – many rich countries and multinational corporations also engage in corrupt practices – which fuels the problem in the first place.

Should all international aid go to charities, rather than governments?

While the work of international development charities such as Action-Aid can improve the lives of millions of people, money from charities alone is not enough to solve all the problems within developing countries. To improve the lives of whole countries or regions, and to sustain this in the long term, governments must play a key role in providing health and education services – creating their own path out of poverty.

What does better aid mean?

Better quality aid means aid that is truly targeted at improving the situation of the poorest and most excluded within societies. At present, too much aid fails to reduce poverty because it never leaves the donor country, damaging strings are attached to it, and rich countries don't properly coordinate the aid they give. Good quality aid supports the development priorities that poor countries identify for themselves. It is provided on a stable basis over a number of years so that countries can plan for the long term. Developing countries can spend it on achieving their development priorities in the way they decide is most useful – free from political interference from donor governments. More aid can lift millions out of poverty – but only when it is good quality.

Haven't almost all of poor countries debts been cancelled already?

Since the Jubilee 2000 campaign, and particularly during Make Poverty History in 2005, progress was made in cancelling the debts of poor countries. After the G8 summit in Gleneagles 20 countries received debt cancellation totalling $38 billion. However, poor countries still owe rich nations over $300 billion – so there is much more to do before all the debt is cancelled.

⇨ The above information is reprinted with kind permission from ActionAid. Visit www.actionaid.org.uk for more information.

© ActionAid

Paying for poverty

Edmund Woodfield considers why we should spend our hard-earned money helping people in other countries

In the words of Benjamin Franklin, 'In this world nothing can be said to be certain, except death and taxes.' But, when it comes to what the government spends our taxes on, a lot of people aren't convinced international development should be a priority. The reasoning behind this is simple: British people pay these taxes and British people should benefit from them.

Nevertheless, for many people, there is a moral imperative to help those who are not as fortunate as we are. It's hard to see a video of children dying of starvation and say that it's not up to us to do anything about it. We have a duty to the rest of humanity to fight against such poverty and it doesn't matter whether it's on our doorstep or thousands of miles away.

Perhaps people oppose spending money on international development because they overestimate what proportion of our income is spent on foreign aid. In 2005, Gallup International polled Americans to see how much aid they thought

America gave as a proportion of its income. Although the actual figure was 0.22% (one of the lowest amongst developed countries) 18% of those polled chose ranges from 5% to over 25%. If I thought more than a quarter of my country's money was being spent on overseas development I'd be worried about the results it's currently achieving. I think most people would agree that it's reasonable to be spending more than the 0.52% the UK spent in 2006.

Another reason people give for being suspicious of international aid is that the money goes to corrupt regimes. I'd be a fool if I claimed that corruption is not a problem, but governments and international organisations are aware of the issues involved and how to deal with them. The fact is that if we were able to account for every penny spent on aid, it would be because it had all been spent on accountants. A sensible balance needs to be found, and in my view, most of the time we get it right.

Finally, international development is important because our world is

now such a small place. A crisis in a faraway country leaves traces around the globe. Poverty can result in conflicts, refugee crises and increasing corruption. Instead of waiting to deal with the consequences of poverty, we should be ready to deal with the causes, which in the long run will be a better use of our resources.

So the next time someone asks you why our taxes and charity should go towards alleviating poverty in other nations, you have three weapons: their conscience, the statistics and their own self-interest.
25 October 2007

⇨ The article on this page, from *Paying for Poverty* www.oxfam.org.uk/ generationwhy/yoursay/articles/ yoursay259.htm, is reproduced with the permission of Oxfam GB, Oxfam House, John Smith Drive, Cowley, Oxford OX4 2JY, UK www. oxfam.org.uk. Oxfam GB does not necessarily endorse any text or activities that accompany the materials.

© Oxfam

Public attitudes to aid

Information from ActionAid

About the poll

ActionAid commissioned this poll as a contribution to an ongoing discussion about how best to make sure the public are engaged and informed about aid. In particular, we wanted to know more about how the public views aid quality issues, which ActionAid believes are central to making aid an effective contribution to the fight against poverty.

In designing the poll, we examined and built on existing polling data, in particular the Office of National Statistics' yearly 'Public attitudes

to development' survey. ICM interviewed a random sample of 1009 adults aged 18+ by telephone across the UK between 19th and 20th December 2006.

Main findings
1. Public support for aid is high and more robust than might be assumed
Our findings show that the public has an astonishingly high estimation of how much public money is being spent on overseas aid. The mean average estimate for the proportion of

government spending accounted for by aid was 18.55%. The actual figure is only 1.3%. Even accounting for the fact that respondents weren't given a yardstick against which to estimate, only 19% guessed between 1 and 2%. Almost a quarter (24%) guessed between 3 and 10% and another quarter guessed more than 10%. As we might expect, there were substantial differences across class, gender and age, but all categories over-estimated by a considerable amount.

Despite this, our poll shows – as previous polls have – a very high level of support for current aid expenditure, and for the government's intention to increase aid. When told that 1.3% or £4.4billion was the correct figure, almost three-quarters – 72% – judged this 'about right' or too little. A substantial majority were in favour when told that the government plans to increase aid in order to help meet the Millennium Development Goals. There were differences across age and class, but all categories had a majority in support of aid, and of the government's intention to increase it.

Interestingly, almost three-quarters – 74% – think aid should increase even if every penny can't be accounted for, suggesting that this support is quite robust.

2. The public are concerned about aid quality

The poll showed a high level of scepticism about the UK government's efforts to use its aid effectively. A majority – 54% – 'tended to' or 'strongly disagreed' that the UK government pays enough attention to ensuring that its aid is used effectively. This throws the early findings into interesting relief – the public strongly supports government aid, even though they are highly sceptical about how much importance the government attaches to aid effectiveness: more evidence that support for aid is robust.

3. Aid sceptics could be won over by improvements to quality

The 'aid sceptics' – those who opposed the government's plans to increase aid – were asked why they did so. The majority – 52% – said that 'we should spend the money in this country, not overseas'. Other popular answers were: 'the aid won't get through to the poor – it is lost to corruption' (22%) and 'the aid will be wasted on bureaucracy & expensive consultants' (12%).

Of course, as each respondent could only select one answer, this does not suggest that these were the only reasons they opposed aid increases, but it does indicate that corruption may not dominate the public's list of concerns in the way that some have suggested.

Furthermore, a majority (57%) of these aid sceptics said they would support the increases 'if the aid provided by the UK could be fully accounted for and guaranteed to help the poorest'.

4. More public discussion of aid would be welcomed

A majority – 56% – thought there was 'too little' public discussion of aid, with only 9% saying there was 'too much'.
February 2007

⇨ The above information is reprinted with kind permission from ActionAid. Visit www.actionaid.org.uk for more.
© *ActionAid*

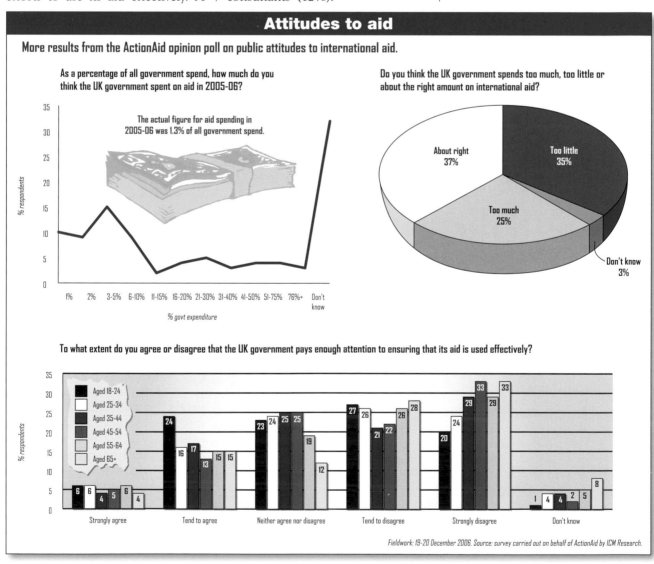

Attitudes to aid

More results from the ActionAid opinion poll on public attitudes to international aid.

As a percentage of all government spend, how much do you think the UK government spent on aid in 2005-06?

The actual figure for aid spending in 2005-06 was 1.3% of all government spend.

% respondents / % govt expenditure
1% 2% 3-5% 6-10% 11-15% 16-20% 21-30% 31-40% 41-50% 51-75% 76%+ Don't know

Do you think the UK government spends too much, too little or about the right amount on international aid?

- About right 37%
- Too little 35%
- Too much 25%
- Don't know 3%

To what extent do you agree or disagree that the UK government pays enough attention to ensuring that its aid is used effectively?

- Aged 18-24
- Aged 25-34
- Aged 35-44
- Aged 45-54
- Aged 55-64
- Aged 65+

Fieldwork: 19-20 December 2006. Source: survey carried out on behalf of ActionAid by ICM Research.

Only trade can solve global poverty

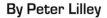

By Peter Lilley

People have strangely mixed reactions about aid for developing countries.

Asked by pollsters whether they think 'aid is a good thing and should be increased' or 'aid is largely wasted and stolen', the largest group of replies were not those who said yes to the first question, nor yes to the second, but those who said yes to both.

The policy group on global poverty, which David Cameron asked me to chair, concluded that people are right to want more aid.

And they are right to be concerned about making sure it is effective and gets through to the poor. Most of our report is about how to achieve those aims.

But aid alone is not enough.

Even if the rich countries fulfil their pledges to increase aid, the total amount will still be inadequate to finance all the health, education, nutrition, water and sanitation that people living on the edge of survival need.

Above all, they need economic growth to boost their incomes. And trade is the great dynamo of growth.

So we want to see a campaign to achieve for developing countries' trade what Drop the Debt and Make Poverty History have done for debt relief and aid.

The aim should be to give all low-income countries real trade opportunities with the developed world – that is why we call the campaign 'Real Trade'.

We hope there will be popular pressure on governments in the EU and other rich countries to put a real trade package at the heart of a revived Doha round or, if it fails, in its place.

In our view, Real Trade would require rich countries to do five things: open their markets unilaterally to the products of all low-income countries; liberalise the 'rules of origin' that result in 40 per cent of imports that should enter Europe tariff-free paying duties; give incentives to reduce the high tariff barriers between developing countries; abolish export subsidies that damage Third World agriculture; and give more Aid for Trade to help poor countries develop their exports.

> ## There has been a tendency to sweep the issue of corruption under the carpet for fear it will undermine taxpayers' support for aid

We also want to see more emphasis on economic growth in aid programmes. The proportion of OECD donors' aid spent on infrastructure has fallen by two-thirds and that on agriculture by even more over two decades.

Yet three-quarters of the world's poor depend on agriculture and one of the great successes of aid was the Green Revolution in Asia, which tripled output in irrigated farming.

We praise Britain's Department for International Development (DfID) as one of the best in the world, but if it is to become more growth-oriented it will need to recruit people with business experience, and its staff working in developing countries will need to spend more than four days a year outside the capital.

There has been a tendency to sweep the issue of corruption under the carpet for fear it will undermine taxpayers' support for aid.

We argue that it must be brought into the daylight, since sunshine is the best disinfectant and transparency is the best way to tackle corruption.

So Britain should require recipient governments to publish funds allocated to individual schools, clinics etc. and insist on reliable auditing. We recommend public expenditure tracking surveys to track how much money allocated from the central budget actually reaches the schools and other projects.

One such survey in Honduras followed the money allocated by central government for teachers' salaries through the government system to a sample of schools and counted how many teachers were actually teaching in the classroom.

It found that – because of leakages en route, the employment of phantom teachers, and the non-appearance of real teachers who had other jobs – only 20 per cent of allocated funds ended up paying for teachers in the classroom.

However, once each school was notified of the amount due to it, pressure from parents ensured that the position improved. A later study showed that 80 per cent of the money now reached the classroom.

British officials should not be reticent in highlighting evidence of corruption, since this strengthens the hands of local campaigners. Despite the DfID's declared policy of zero tolerance, it has not pursued a single case of governmental corruption of late.

The effectiveness of aid is undermined not just by poor governance within developing countries, but also by poor governance by donors: duplication, unreliability, top-down decision making and emphasis on aid inputs.

In 2001, Tanzania had to produce more than 2,400 reports to donors, and government officials met more than 1,000 donor delegations.

In Vietnam, it took donors 18 months and the time of 150 government workers just to buy five vehicles for a forestry programme.

We advocate creating partnership trusts in each country to pool the aid efforts of as many donors as possible.

Ideally the funds will handle both budget/programme support and most project finance. And we want to see a global donor index measuring each donor's performance to press them to follow best practice.

Aid is all too often initiated from the top down. To harness the knowledge, experience and self-interest of people in each developing country, we recommend establishing demand-led funds, which will invite not just governments but also NGOs, local civic groups and private companies to submit proposals.

The funds will finance the best as long as they have performance measures and independent auditing.

I know some people argue that 'charity begins at home'. True: but it should not end there.

When millions of children go to bed hungry and we can do something about it, we cannot pass by on the other side of the world. And poverty affects our security and prosperity as well as our humanity.

The UN High Commissioner for Refugees has warned of waves of immigration from an arc of unstable and fragile states unless more is done to rebuild their homelands.

Those who believe that current pressures go beyond what is economically or socially acceptable need to take heed.

Compassion and self-interest mean we must bring a new energy to getting our aid, trade and development policies right. I hope this report will help a future Conservative government to do so.
⇨ *Peter Lilley chairs the Conservatives' globalisation and global poverty policy group 24 July 2007*
© *Telegraph Group Limited, London 2008*

How foreign aid can damage the poorest

Philip Booth on development aid in the *Catholic Herald*

Since the mid twentieth century, Catholic social teaching has often promoted government-to-government aid from rich to poor countries. *Populorum progressio* perhaps marked the high water mark of the promotion of this policy. It would, though, be foolish to promote development aid if it were not possible to show that it improved the chances of development of the poorest people. When *Populorum progressio* was written, there was a broad consensus that the causes of poverty in the under-developed world were such that poverty could be alleviated by aid. There is now no such consensus.

To begin with, it is worth noting that the under-developed world has become much smaller in the last 40 years as many countries have developed without aid. This process of development, along with globalisation, has done much to reduce relative and absolute poverty. The gap between many formerly poor countries that have recently seen rapid growth and those countries that have been relatively well off for many decades has narrowed significantly. Over half the world's population now lives in 40 countries that are growing at more than 7% per year. Development is happening and is benefiting huge numbers of previously-poor people.

Aid rewards the governing elites in those countries where those elites keep their people poor

That said, there remains dire poverty. Is aid the solution to under-development today? There are two sets of problems with aid: the first set is essentially political or institutional and the second macro-economic.

The provision of development aid is, by nature, a top-down process. Aid therefore rewards the governing elites in those countries where those elites keep their people poor. Aid also makes it more likely that incompetent, corrupt or brutal government will survive because aid provides the resources that enable poor or unjust government to perpetuate itself. Frequently, such governments have, of course, pursued policies that have included the persecution or expulsion of the most productive ethnic groups in society.

Furthermore, aid directs entrepreneurial activity perversely. In many African countries aid is a very significant proportion of national income. Educated people within a country that receives large amounts of aid have a strong incentive to direct their efforts upwards, towards government, to become beneficiaries of aid-financed projects, instead of attempting to raise their material position through business and entrepreneurship. On a wider scale, the greater the proportion of national income and wealth that is controlled by government, the greater is the incentive for ethnic groups to engage in conflict to try to control government.

There is also a tendency for aid not to be used for its intended purpose, such as health and education, but, instead, to be used to meet the aims of governing elites. Even if aid is used for its intended purposes, in order to provide evidence for donors, it can displace investment that otherwise would have taken place in these sectors, including private sector investment. The additional resources are then, in effect, used for government consumption. A 2004 survey tracked spending by the government of Chad intended for rural hospital projects. Only 1% of money intended to be spent on the projects reached the hospitals. It is therefore not surprising that about 40% of Africa's military spending is inadvertently financed by aid.

All these problems encourage corruption in public life because government functionaries and ministers have relatively more power and economic resources that they can use for preferment.

Aid can also have seriously problematic macro-economic effects which are well researched. These effects are worse, ironically, the better aid money is spent. Aid spent on investment projects can lower the rate of return from investment projects financed by private saving and thus reduce saving and investment. Aid also raises the exchange rate, making life more difficult for exporters. These effects can be alleviated if developing countries in receipt of aid liberalise foreign trade. As it happens, trade liberalisation is also very helpful in reducing opportunities for corruption.

It is not surprising, then, that there appears to be a negative relationship between aid and economic growth. In total in the 30 years from 1970, Africa received $400bn of aid, under different regimes, tied to different forms of economic policy and reform, yet it is difficult to find any evidence of a single country developing because of aid. Even aid proponent Paul Collier cautions that

increases in aid from current levels may be counter-productive because of rapidly diminishing returns once aid is a high proportion of a country's budget.

It is becoming increasingly clear that the basic precondition for development is good governance, including the enforcement of private property, freedom of contract, enforcement of contracts, the rule of law, the authority of law and the absence of corruption. This list is not exhaustive, of course. It appears that, if these preconditions are present, development and growth will generally follow. Indeed, a recent study showed how the top twenty-four countries in the world, ranked by quality of their legal systems, had average growth of nearly ten times that of the bottom twenty-one countries. Development is impossible without the basic legal structures necessary for free economic activity but flourishes when the institutional environment is favourable.

This is an important result because the main concern of aid sceptics is that aid undermines the development of good governance. But, can we have smarter aid? Can we do better in the future?

More aid could be administered through charities, businesses and other private bodies. Although there is then a potential problem that aid agencies who receive government funds, such as our own Cafod, can become politicised, on balance this is probably a better approach.

Paul Collier argues that aid must be tied to a commitment to conflict resolution and can be used very effectively to provide technical assistance in a reform programme. The West is wary of conflict resolution unless it just involves a few blue-bereted UN troops being driven round in trucks. Real life conflict resolution in very poor countries can be a messy job but can be very helpful to the country concerned. Technical assistance sounds boring and British Ministers like to be seen surrounded by lots of singing children whilst opening aid-financed schools. But, education and healthcare should perhaps be left to charities and other private

bodies; government aid might be better used providing technical help to try to create institutions of good governance.

This article is the summary of a talk given at the Pontifical Athenaeum Regina Apostolorum in Rome a few weeks ago. Interestingly, many of the seminarians and priests from Africa who were there not only welcomed the message but asked why Western governments were not doing more to end corruption and oppression in African countries. Ironically, if I had given the talk to a white middle-class Justice and Peace group down in the South East of England, I might have been lucky to get out alive. The reality is that the consensus amongst economists on which *Populorum progressio* was founded is broken. Christians who are aid proponents should be careful how they promote their opinions. They should do so with less confidence and fervour. In this area of development aid, we need to muddle through, recognising the seriousness of the problems we seek to address but also the fact that aid-driven solutions seem to have had effects that range from doing a little good to much harm.

By Professor Philip Booth, Editorial and Programme Director, Institute of Economic Affairs
28 March 2008

⇨ The above information is re-printed with kind permission from the Institute of Economic Affairs and was first published in the *Catholic Herald* on 28 March 2008. Visit www. iea.org.uk for more information.
© *Institute of Economic Affairs/Catholic Herald*

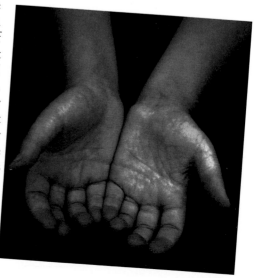

⇨ In 2005/06, 12.7 million people in the UK (22 per cent) were income poor, living in households with below 60 per cent of the median income after housing costs. Though in recent years this has been falling, in 2005/06 it rose. In 1979, 15 per cent were in this position. (page 1)

⇨ The primary cause of poverty is inadequate income, arising primarily from worklessness, and inadequate wages and benefits. (page 2)

⇨ People in Britain are concerned about inequality, but they are less likely to support government interventions designed to tackle poverty or redistribute income than they were 20 years ago. Indeed, according to the latest British Social Attitudes report, published by NatCen, one in four people think that poverty is due to laziness or lack of willpower, up from one in five in 1986. (page 3)

⇨ New research charting the attitudes of children to poverty in Britain shows that nearly half of all young people think missing out on school trips or not having the correct school uniform are the most telling indicators of being poor. (page 4)

⇨ Five million working people face poverty and exclusion as they are being ignored by government and business, according to a new report. (page 5)

⇨ Nearly three out of four people (74%) think that income differences in Britain are too large and seven in ten (69%) believe that parents' income plays too big a part in determining children's life chances. (page 7)

⇨ According to members of the public, a single person in Britain today needs to earn at least £13,400 a year before tax to afford a basic but acceptable standard of living. (page 8)

⇨ There are an estimated three million disabled people living in relative poverty in the UK. (page 10)

⇨ Barnardo's estimates that the costs to the UK economy in not tackling child poverty total more than £40 billion a year. (page 11)

⇨ A new report by Save the Children reveals that as many as 2.3 million people in the UK on low incomes are being forced to take out high-interest loans at rates topping 183% APR – many simply to provide essentials for their children. (page 12)

⇨ 41 per cent of survey respondents thought there was very little real child poverty in Britain today; 53 per cent thought there was quite a lot. (page 14)

⇨ Four out of ten (39%) of children in poverty are in single-mother households. (page 15)

⇨ Three out of four parents and guardians find meeting their child's school costs 'very' or 'quite' difficult, according to a new survey. (page 16)

⇨ By the time they move to secondary school poorer children are on average two years behind better-off children. (page 18)

⇨ 19% of adults with children aged 17 or under have suffered from cold homes because of the cost of energy. 15% of households have cut back on food, and the same proportion has had to cut back on essential clothing in order to pay fuel bills. (page 22)

⇨ The DWP estimates that up to £9.4 billion is not being claimed in means-tested benefits by those who are entitled to it. (page 24)

⇨ Of the world's 6.1 billion people, some 1.1 billion live in extreme poverty. (page 25)

⇨ Globally, people are described as living in poverty if they have less than US$1 a day to live on. (page 28)

⇨ 852 million people do not have enough to eat, 1.3 billion have no safe water, 2 billion have no access to electricity and 3 billion have no sanitation. (page 29)

⇨ Altogether, developing countries pay around £600 million every day to the rich world. For every £1 that poor countries receive in aid, they pay out more than £2 in debt service. (page 33)

⇨ The majority of aid to developing countries comes from the governments of wealthy countries. The internationally agreed target for how much a government should give in aid is 0.7% of gross national income – although only a few countries have reached this level. (page 34)

⇨ ActionAid findings show that the public has an astonishingly high estimation of how much UK public money is being spent on overseas aid. The mean average estimate for the proportion of government spending accounted for by aid was 18.55%. The actual figure is only 1.3%. (page 35)

⇨ The ActionAid poll showed a high level of scepticism about the UK government's efforts to use its aid effectively. A majority – 54% – 'tended to' or 'strongly disagreed' that the UK government pays enough attention to ensuring that its aid is used effectively. (page 36)

GLOSSARY

Affluence
Wealth; abundance of money or valuable resources.

APR
Annual Percentage Rate. The annual rate of interest which must be paid on a loan.

Benefits
We use the term 'state benefits' to describe any money that is given to us by the government. Benefits are paid to any member of the public, who may need extra money to help them meet the costs of everyday living.

Downward mobility
An adult who finds themselves living in a household which is relatively worse off than the one in which they grew up is said to have been downwardly mobile.

Extreme poverty
With reference to global poverty, this term refers to an inability to meet even the most basic survival needs (food, water, housing).

Free trade
An economic policy which promotes the free movement of goods and services between countries and the elimination of restrictions to trading between nations, such as import and export tariffs.

Fair trade
A movement which advocates fair prices, improved working conditions and better trade terms for producers in developing countries. Exports from developing countries that have been certified Fairtrade, which include products such as coffee, cocoa and bananas, carry the Fairtrade mark.

Fuel poverty
An individual's inability to provide adequate heating for their household due to the costs involved.

Gross Domestic Product (GDP)
The value of all the goods and services produced in a country in a year.

Income
The sum of all money entering a household.

International aid
Aid is economic assistance provided by the governments of rich countries to poorer countries in order to help them achieve a humanitarian goal (to alleviate poverty or hunger, for example). The UK currently allocates 1.3% of government spending for overseas aid.

Means-tested
If something is means-tested, it is only paid out if certain conditions are met relating to an individual's financial situation. Means-tested benefits, for example, will be paid only to those applicants whose income falls below a certain level.

Millennium Development Goals
In 2000, world leaders decided that they needed a strategy to tackle poverty. They set and agreed targets, which are called the Millennium Development Goals. Goal 1 aims to eradicate extreme poverty and hunger, with a target of halving 1990 levels of poverty and hunger by 2015.

Moderate poverty
With reference to global poverty, this term is applied to people who can meet their basic needs (food, water, housing), but who lack the resources to improve their lives.

National debt
The national debt is the amount of money owed by a country's government to other countries and international financial institutions. Developing countries, containing some of the world's poorest people, currently pay around £600 million every day to the rich world in debt repayments.

Poverty
Peter Townsend offers this definition of poverty: 'Individuals, families and groups in the population can be said to be in poverty when they lack the resources to obtain the types of diet, participate in the activities, and have the living conditions and amenities which are customary, or are at least widely encouraged and approved, in the societies in which they belong.'

Poverty line
The poverty line is the income level below which an individual can be said to be living in poverty. In the UK, the poverty line is defined as 60 per cent of the median household income, adjusted for household composition. 22 per cent of people in the UK (12.7 million) fell into this category in 2005/06. Globally speaking, people are defined as living in absolute poverty if they have less than $1 (USD) a day to live on. Over a billion people worldwide fall into this category.

Social exclusion
Social exclusion refers to a lack of access to resources, possessions and activities which most members of society take for granted, thereby affecting an individual's quality of life. It is not simply about income poverty: it is about being excluded from the mainstream of society.

INDEX

Additional Resources

Other Issues titles

If you are interested in researching further some of the issues raised in *Poverty and Exclusion*, you may like to read the following titles in the **Issues** series:

⇨ Vol. 159 *An Ageing Population* (ISBN 978 1 86168 452 3)

⇨ Vol. 157 *The Problem of Globalisation* (ISBN 978 1 86168 444 8)

⇨ Vol. 156 *Travel and Tourism* (ISBN 978 1 86168 443 1)

⇨ Vol. 154 *The Gender Gap* (ISBN 978 1 86168 441 7)

⇨ Vol. 150 *Migration and Population* (ISBN 978 1 86168 423 3)

⇨ Vol. 149 *A Classless Society?* (ISBN 978 1 86168 422 6)

⇨ Vol. 139 *The Education Problem* (ISBN 978 1 86168 391 5)

⇨ Vol. 137 *Crime and Anti-Social Behaviour* (ISBN 978 1 86168 389 2)

⇨ Vol. 134 *Customers and Consumerism* (ISBN 978 1 86168 386 1)

⇨ Vol. 133 *Teen Pregnancy and Lone Parents* (ISBN 978 1 86168 379 3)

⇨ Vol. 130 *Homelessness* (ISBN 978 1 86168 376 2)

⇨ Vol. 120 *The Human Rights Issue* (ISBN 978 1 86168 353 3)

⇨ Vol. 107 *Work Issues* (ISBN 978 1 86168 327 4)

⇨ Vol. 89 *Refugees* (ISBN 978 1 86168 290 1)

⇨ Vol. 85 *The Housing Crisis* (ISBN 978 1 86168 280 2)

⇨ Vol. 74 *Money Matters* (ISBN 978 1 86168 263 5)

For more information about these titles, visit our website at www.independence.co.uk/publicationslist

Useful organisations

You may find the websites of the following organisations useful for further research:

⇨ **ActionAid:** www.actionaid.org.uk

⇨ **Barnardo's:** www.barnardos.org.uk

⇨ **Campaign to End Child Poverty:** www.endchildpoverty.org.uk

⇨ **Child Poverty Action Group:** www.cpag.org.uk

⇨ **Christian Aid:** www.christianaid.org.uk

⇨ **Citizens Advice Bureau:** www.citizensadvice.org.uk

⇨ **Department for Work and Pensions:** www.dwp.gov.uk

⇨ **Fawcett Society:** www.fawcettsociety.org.uk

⇨ **Frank Buttle Trust:** www.buttletrust.org

⇨ **Institute of Economic Affairs:** www.iea.org.uk

⇨ **Institute for Social and Economic Research:** www.iser.essex.ac.uk

⇨ **Joseph Rowntree Foundation:** www.jrf.org.uk

⇨ **Jubilee Debt Campaign:** www.jubileedebtcampaign.org.uk

⇨ **NatCen:** www.natcen.ac.uk

⇨ **National Consumer Council:** www.ncc.org.uk

⇨ **Oxfam:** www.oxfam.org.uk

⇨ **politics.co.uk:** www.politics.co.uk

⇨ **The Poverty Site:** www.poverty.org.uk

⇨ **Save the Children:** www.savethechildren.org.uk

⇨ **Sutton Trust:** www.suttontrust.com

⇨ **World Vision:** www.worldvision.org.uk

ACKNOWLEDGEMENTS

The publisher is grateful for permission to reproduce the following material.

While every care has been taken to trace and acknowledge copyright, the publisher tenders its apology for any accidental infringement or where copyright has proved untraceable. The publisher would be pleased to come to a suitable arrangement in any such case with the rightful owner.

Chapter One: Poverty in the UK

Poverty: the facts, © Child Poverty Action Group, *Britons lose sympathy for the poor*, © NatCen, *Monitoring poverty and social exclusion*, © New Policy Institute, *Missing school trips makes you poor, say British kids*, © Community Services Volunteers/Campaign to End Child Poverty, *Britain's forgotten poor*, © National Consumer Council, *Household income*, © Crown copyright is reproduced with the permission of Her Majesty's Stationery Office, *Wage gap too large, say three out of four Britons*, © Sutton Trust, *Minimum living standards*, © Joseph Rowntree Foundation, *Growing inequality*, © University of Essex, *Disabled people and poverty*, © Leonard Cheshire Disability, *Paying the price of poverty*, © Barnardo's, *Poverty and debt*, © Save the Children, *Living with hardship 24/7*, © Frank Buttle Trust, *Public attitudes to child poverty*, © Crown copyright is reproduced with the permission of Her Majesty's Stationery Office, *Keeping mum*, © Fawcett Society, *The cost of education*, © Citizens Advice Bureau, *Social exclusion and education*, © Joseph Rowntree Foundation, *2 skint 4 school*, © Child Poverty Action Group, *Child poverty: true or false?*, © Save the Children, *Disadvantage and achievement*, © Institute of Education, University of London, *Mind the gap*, © Guardian Newspapers Ltd, *1 in 5 families can't afford heating*, © Save the Children, *What are benefits?*, © askcab, *Benefit claims and poverty*, © Child Poverty Action Group, *Welfare shake-up scraps incapacity benefit*, © politics.co.uk.

Chapter Two: Global Poverty

Poverty: a 10-minute guide, © World Vision, *Life on $1 a day*, © Christian Aid, *Global poverty*, © World Vision UK, *Facts and figures*, © Christian Aid, *Poverty, hunger and disease*, © Guardian Newspapers Ltd, *It's a question of debt*, © Jubilee Debt Campaign, *Aid questions and answers*, © ActionAid, *Paying for poverty*, © Oxfam, *Public attitudes to aid*, © ActionAid, *Only trade can solve global poverty*, © Telegraph Group Ltd, *How foreign aid can damage the poorest*, © Institute of Economic Affairs/Catholic Herald.

Photographs

Flickr: pages 13 (Paul Downey); 18 (Belinda Hankins Miller); 27 (Pam Roth); 30 (Angela Sevin).
Stock Xchng: pages 2, 39 (Sophie); 4 (Sanja Gjenero); 5 (Matthew Bowden); 14 (Nimalan Tharmalingam); 15 (Jason Nelson); 16 (Steve Woods); 33 (Jon Ng); 37 (Dani Simmonds).

Illustrations

Pages 7, 12, 25: Angelo Madrid; pages 9, 20, 31: Simon Kneebone; pages 10, 23: Bev Aisbett; pages 11, 21, 34: Don Hatcher.

Additional editorial by Claire Owen, on behalf of Independence Educational Publishers.

And with thanks to the team: Mary Chapman, Sandra Dennis, Claire Owen and Jan Sunderland.

Lisa Firth
Cambridge
September, 2008